Published by:

Self Publishing

United States

Dedication

To all Nigerian youths who work to reduce challenges among themselves, standing up for what is right, and bringing in good ideas that will help through positive development of the citizens of the country.

Acknowledgements

To Almighty God

My first acknowledgement goes to the Great Immortality of all immortals. He cannot be seen but can be felt. On my own I cannot do anything. God is the one that inspires and he inspired me before I could write on this book title.

To Muhammed Abdullahi Tosin

There are hidden talents in some persons yet to be discovered by people that possess such talents. Sometimes someone somewhere needs to touch these potentials before they can shine bright for people to see and benefit from them. Mr Muhammed Abdullahi Tosin touched the writing potential in me and it has shine out to the entire world. My written articles and books which have been read for over 1.7 million times by people from different parts of the world are made possible by you.

I did not know I could write until you organized essay contest in

2013 for students in different tertiary institutions in Nigeria. I participated in the contest and came out second nationwide after judgement. You made me discover the potential that has not been tapped into since birth. And from that day, I became an author that has attracted people both locally and internationally. I acknowledge your good heart dear Tosin.

To Amazon

My sincere gratitude goes to Jeff Bezos, the CEO of Amazon and the world richest man in 2018, for creating a platform where independent authors from different parts of the world publish their works to global market. I also acknowledge the entire Amazon team.

Contents

Chapter 3...157

Drug abuse among Nigerian Youths

Chapter 4...215

Young Fraudsters in Nigeria (Yahoo or G

Boys)

Chapter 1

Introduction to Youth Challenges in Nigeria

There is a country called Nigeria. This country is made up of vibrant young men and women. Some members of this country whom are within certain age range are ready to do anything for money. They are hungry.

What statistics of Nigerian youths makes up the population of the country? Out of the 197,457,502 (approximately 197 million) total

1

Nigeria population in 2018, 33,652,424 of them are youths. From the calculation, it shows that approximately 17% of Nigerian population are youths. According to National Youth Policy, youth in Nigeria includes citizens of the Federal Republic of Nigeria aged 18–35 years. The definition of a youth is dependent on location and the above is as related to Nigeria.

Youths in the Federal Republic of Nigeria have been facing many issues in the country. In the area of politics, the young men and women in the country have been denied their right in getting involved. The wicked and shameless old men who feel they are almighty have been recycling themselves in top positions as far as politics in the country is concerned. The young are seriously giving up in the struggle to take over power in the country.

The statistics of Nigerian youths in politics in the Federal Republic of Nigeria is very small. It is very small to the extent that some of the youths ask themselves if they are really part of the country. Some of them have great ideas that will take the country to standard level but are not given the opportunity instead old men who suppose to be in their homes resting are occupying top political positions in the country.

As of the time of initiation of this book writing, in October of the year 2018, the President of the Federal Republic of Nigeria is 75 years and still occupying position instead of resting at this old age. The worst of it all is that he is still agitating for second tenure which is another 4 years in office. Nigeria as a country has spent much money on the health status of this president. Instead of using the money to develop the country, it is spent on a man that puts himself into unnecessary pressure.

In January 20, 2017, President Buhari left the country to London for medical treatment with the hope of returning to the country on February 6, 2018 but the return was extended indefinitely when the initial due date reached because he needed more time. For that duration, the government of the country spent a lot of money not only on his health alone but also in maintaining the private jet he travelled with. It was a shame that in the scarcity of money in the country, it was wasted.

During his stay in London which involved burning lot of cash, a Nigerian voice out through twitter handle. Quoting him through the publication of Guardian News, he lamented, "Nigerian, Samuel Philip @ The_improviser stoked controversy. His 9.48 am tweet yesterday morning instantly got 30 retweets. "If Buhari's jet is still in London waiting to bring him back it must have amassed a lot of parking cost," he said, with Steven Jeff Sakada @ sakalajeff retweeting: "Yep, landing fees for a jumbo jet liner are up to 1000 pounds a day at Heathrow." Samuel Philips responds: "Tax payers' money or the President earns that much?" Imagine that kind of money per day, how much would he have spent just for his jet packing for the whole of his stay in London. If we go by the calculation from the quote, it means that the government spent 103000 pounds for the packing space of the jet alone. This is for staying for 103 days.

Again, according to Guardian Nigerian News, Buhari may have spent £2000 on private treatment in London. The exact amount spent on medical is not known as the hospital refused to make this known to the public. The possibility of a young president falling sick that will make him or her spend much on hospital abroad is very slim.

Youth unemployment is a crucial topic that has been occupying top pages in both local and international press companies for a long time now. Nigerian youths also take part as people that have been eating from this bitter cake. In fact, youths in Nigeria are one of the most affected by unemployment challenge globally. They are finding it difficult to cope. Many Nigerian youths that graduated from institutions of higher learning are finding it difficult to make impact in their society with what they studied in the universities and colleges. But any youth that think outside the box irrespective of his or her course of study will succeed.

In internet scam, Nigeria rank very high. Some Nigerian youths have taken internet scam as means of survival in life. As a confirmation, Nigeria as a country ranked 3rd in global internet crimes in the year 2017 (NCC 2017). Hacking of social media accounts of people including Facebook, and Instagram is a common culture being practiced by Nigerian youths. Some have taken fraud as their fulltime job.

It is not advisable for social media users to use weak passwords like phone numbers during creation of their social media site accounts. The reason is because these guys called Yahoo or G boys can easily tamper with such accounts. Though there are other tricks used by these young men and ladies in the society but more will be discussed on that in a separate chapter.

The abuse of drugs among the youths in Nigeria is alarming. It is becoming so pronounced to the extent that those that are not partakers are seen as weak. But those that have such philosophy are weak intellectually. They are sick unknowing to them. They abuse these drugs daily without considering the side effects of what they are getting themselves into. It is pitiable to see how some Nigerian youths behave when they get high due to abuse of the drugs they take.

To curb this abuse to some extent, Nigerian government recently took a bold step but that was not enough. Both the parents and more experienced adults in the society still need to contribute practically to see how this challenge can be drastically reduced to some extent. Leaving the fight only for the government of Nigeria may not show great effective outcome.

Irrespective of the fact that there are youth groups established by the governments of the country to address Nigerian youth challenges, they are not enough. We will be discussing these youth groups in details in a separate chapter. But, of a truth, empowering of Nigerian youths by non-governmental organizations and individuals can go a long way to solve the challenges faced by the youths nationwide. It is not one man's thing; otherwise we will end up achieving nothing at the end. Tony Elumelu Foundation for instance has helped many Nigerians achieve their goals in life. If Nigeria has about 50 of her citizens that will follow the footstep of this great philanthropist and do the same, the citizens issues as well as the youth challenges will reduce drastically with respect to time. Tony has been imparting into the lives of the citizens of the country in a very outstanding way.

The Tony Elumelu Foundation is an African non-profit organization founded in 2010 by Tony O. Elumelu and headquartered in Lagos, Nigeria, based on his belief that, with the right support, entrepreneurs can be empowered to contribute meaningfully to Africa's prosperity and social development. The foundation organises yearly competition among African countries and winners with great entrepreneurship ideas are empowered financially by the foundation to start businesses of their own. The work of the great Nigerian has attracted the attention of international bodies.

1.1 Youth Benefits

Irrespective of the challenges that Nigerian youths face in their life struggles, there are still many benefits of being a youth. Any youth that understands these benefits need to fight for his survival irrespective of the ups and downs in the society he or she finds his or herself. The benefits of being a youth are but not limited to:

- It gives members the ability to plan their lives the way they want it

- Enormous strength to carry out one function or the other

- A youth thinks fast. His reasoning can go far beyond what other elderly in the society can think of. Because of this, an idea generated by the youth can keep the world for a very long time

- Youthful age creates avenues for the youths to build good relationships that will take them till their lifetime

- Less financial burden. Unlike married people who think always on how to meet the demands of their family which among them can be huge financial demand, a single youth does not face such challenge. He takes his time to build himself without much pressure. He goes to his work and comes back to manage himself. Even if there is no food in the house, he can sleep till the next day. He has lesser things to think about.

- Youths are fearless. Ever engaged an advanced person in your society and asked him how he usually feels when he was a young man in terms of fear? He can tell you that her fears nothing or less than his current state. As of then, he has nothing like his wife or children to be bothered about.

But as he became full adult, fear began to grip in. He considers his family before he does certain things as a result of fear.

At this point, let's take a look at the view of other authors' on the benefits of being a youth. Their views are not far-fetched from the ones given before. They show close resemblance.

According to Anjali Bhavan, youth is resilient; wounds will heal. You will forget. You will become happy. Our bodies are young and lively; any injury will heal faster than you can even believe. I've seen it with my own eyes, believe me.

Being young means you haven't been disappointed yet. You haven't been thrown asunder, you haven't seen the end of the world yet. There's still place for you to spread your wings and fly - and wear purple robes and rule the world!

You can suit up and be a lawyer, and still have a child-like innocence about you. You will step out into this wondrous, cruel world, and see and feel everything for yourself. Those beautiful and painful experiences will never, ever come by as an adult. It's all in the magic of the novelty, the discovery itself.

You will have your looks, health and time by your side in each and every aspect. You'll have springs in your feet.

Picking from the words of Anjali, she said that youths are resilient. What it implies is that youths have the ability to withstand or recover quickly from difficult conditions. No matter how painful any particular emotional pain seems to be, they will still recover and move on with life.

Also, a young person is not totally disappointed at the young age. If he

11

tried and failed, there are many other opportunities for him to try again and again. Time is still by his side, he keeps trying until he gets it right at the end.

That is why you see some youths dating and breaking up after some time until they get whom will suite them to build a family. But at once out of youthful age, it is usually difficult to have such opportunity again. Youths are free and are happy because they are still single.

There is a saying that health is wealth. Being healthy is important and youths enjoy it most. They do not get trapped by some diseases that affect the adults. They are always sound and healthy.

Also, according to another writer, Peter Bazikos, his views on the benefits of being a youth follow this pattern:

"The blessing of time and being debt free. When you're younger you have more time to do everything you want to do than when you are old in that the older you are, the closer to death's door you are. (I know, morbid is it?)

Also being debt free when you're young, you have little debt, unless you just took about a bunch huge loans. When you're young you don't have to deal with paying off debts and that can help you build savings (unless you take out a lot of debt and you use your savings to cover only a fraction of it).

Also with being young you're less likely to have chronic health issues, but a lot of chronic health issues of today's old folks often seem to come from a bad life style they had when they were younger. In short, you have more time to live and a little bit more to do stuff, have little to no debt (unless you took a huge loan) and you probably have better health now than later."

If you become an adult and have a family of your own, there is usually increase in demand. In this way, you have more financial needs to attend to than when you were a single youth. Your wife and children will be demanding and you have to foot those bills. If the money you have is not enough to take care of the bills, you will be pushed to go for loan. And any one that goes for loan automatically owes. Instead of saving to build one or two projects, you keep on paying debts. Youths do not face challenges of this kind in some cases.

1.2 Nigerian Youths in Politics

Because Nigerian practices a democratic system of government, it is to be a playing ground for both the adults and the young. Political positions also are expected to include both adults and the youths. The mixture of the two in political positions will help the government generate solid ideas that will help in running the affair of the country. Nigerian youths have many sound ideas that can make the country move forward to some extent.

The youths in Nigerian are individuals within the age bracket of 18 and 35. No one should say that a man of 26 years for example cannot execute proper political projects. If Nigerian politicians whom have been occupying many positions even the ones made for the youths think it is by age, a young man of 30 years can handle political position and do that accurately. The problem is with the mindset of old politicians that run political offices in the country. Their thinking abilities are poor.

Because of the attitudes of Nigerians who are enjoying top political positions in the country without having the youths in mind, many Nigerian young men and women have decided not to participate in electoral processes. They feel it is a waste of time and energy for them to go and register for their voters' cards. The youths feel that they vote in the old into some major political positions while they the youths are not considered to even occupy any reasonable positions in the country. They feel disappointed and discouraged with the way political positions are handled in the country.

The way Nigerian youths are treated when it comes to their involvement in politics has attracted the attention of international bodies. They have frown at such behaviour of the Nigerian politicians and Political parties. It is not a healthy way of running democratic or other system of governments and something needs to be done as fast as possible.

European Union (EU) on Thursday decried the shortage of Nigerian youths participating in partisan politics. Mr Ketil Karlsen, Ambassador and Head of the EU Delegation to Nigeria and

ECOWAS, said this during the Independent National Electoral Commission (INEC) Continuous Voter Campus Outreach at University of Abuja. According to Karlsen, for democracy to be representative, it must represent all the demographic population of a country, and the youths are an important case in point. There is a shortage of youth's participation in politics in many countries including Nigeria (Vanguard News 2018).

The bill "not too young to run" which has got very tremendous acceptance among Nigerian citizens caught my attention on TV a few days ago where some known civil society faces talked about the successes recorded in campaigns across the states for passage of the bill and greater space for young people to participate in politics. In summary, the 'not too young to run Bill' seeks to alter some Sections of the 1999 Constitution of the Federal Republic of Nigeria (as amended) to reduce the age of qualification for the office of the President, Governor and membership of the National Assembly. In clear terms, at 25 a Nigerian citizen is qualified to run for Houses of Assembly positions and at 30 one can run for the

Governorship, Senate and Presidency (Vanguard News 2018).

Irrespective of the recent development, can the youths of the country be given the adequate opportunity to participate in the politics of the country? The fact remains that time will tell because the old men in politics in the country are not ready to give way for the younger ones to smell top political positions in the country. As a suggestion, it will be good to make a law that will disqualify people of old age not to hold political positions in the country. The idea of an old man of 75 years to be ruling the country as a president is wrong and not supposed.

Nigerian politics have been about the persons with biggest pockets being brought to power. It has been about the politicians with the high amount of money buying themselves into the political positions in the country. How many Nigerian youths have such amount of money to spend to acquire top political positions? The youths may not have such huge amount of money to spend but can team up to change the trend of things that go on. The right mindset and sound ideology is needed. The youths can use their strength, number and intellect to participate fully in every aspect of Nigeria's electoral process and get what they want. They can establish any young person they want to go if they team up as one.

References

- Anjali .B. and Peter .B. (2016), What are the Advantages/Benefits of being young?, published by Quora Inc, California, United States

- Marcel .M. et al (2017), Nigerians weigh cost of Buhari's medical Vacation Abroad, published by Guardian News, Nigeria

- National Youth Policy (2009), Nigeria 2009 National Youth Policy, published by Knowledge for Health

- NCC (2017), Nigeria ranks 3rd in Global Internet Crimes behind UK, U.S. – NCC, report by Nigerian Communications Commission, published by Premium Times News, Nigeria

- Vanguard News (2018), EU decries low participation of Nigerian youths in politics, published by Vanguard News, 2 Vanguard Avenue Kirikiri canal, Apapa Lagos,P.M.B. 1007 Apapa Lagos

- Ibid (2018), The Youth in Nigeria Politics, published by Vanguard News, 2 Vanguard Avenue Kirikiri canal, Apapa Lagos,P.M.B. 1007 Apapa Lagos

- Worldometers (2018), Nigeria Population, Worldometers publication

Chapter 2

Youth Unemployment in Nigeria

Youth Unemployment Rate in Nigeria increased to 33.10 percent in the third quarter of 2017 from 29.50 percent in the second quarter of 2017. Youth unemployment rate in Nigeria averaged 21.73 percent from 2014 until 2017, reaching an all time high of 33.10 percent in the third quarter of 2017 and a record low of 11.70 percent in the fourth quarter of 2014.

Young men and women in this location are really passing through tough times. They are enduring everyday hoping for better tomorrow. To some of these young men, the better tomorrow they have been waiting for a long time is not coming forth and are getting fed up with everything.

Nigeria's self-deceit, with the policymakers erroneously believes that the current dysfunctional structure of a bloated centre can get us out of the economic wood is robbing our youths of a glorious future. Indeed, the recurring ugly decimal of youth unemployment in Nigeria keeps worsening by the decade calls for serious concern and urgent action (Ayo Oyoze Baje 2018). It is pitiable.

According to Olanrewaju Makinde Hassan, unemployment problem like corrupt practices in Nigeria is a hydra headed problem and thus requires the collective effort of both the private and public sectors and the enabling environment, finance and workable policy framework (Olanrewaju 2014). According to the author, addressing this challenge does not only need the effort of the government alone but general efforts of the citizens of the country.

According to Tony, "youth unemployment occurs when young people are without jobs and have actively sought for job within a short period. It is one of the macro-economic problems which every government is expected to monitor and regulate" (Tony 2017). The term 'macro' can be interchanged with big. So from him, it is a big economic problem.

There are some factors that have resulted to the high increase in the youth unemployment rate in the Federal Republic of Nigeria. The causes are much which among them is corruption, bad leadership, non patriotism, poor knowledge, inadequate planning, poor development of mineral resources, selfishness of the politicians, shallow thinking, bad economy, lack of employable skills, inability to explore agriculture and the rest.

In Europe and the other developed parts of the world, students are happy to graduate from institutions of higher learning because they know they will secure jobs and start making positive impact in there society. But in Nigeria, the breath of the youths cut as they leave their universities. The fear is as a result of the effect of unemployment in the society. That is one of the effects of youth unemployment in Nigeria. The fear of graduating from higher institutions without availability of jobs is one of the effects of youth unemployment in the Federal Republic of Nigeria.

On the other hand, this challenge can be addressed if all and sundry contribute in the fight. The government and the citizens of the country have to work hand in hand. But in all, there is need for sincerity. If the government and the citizens are sincere and are devoted to work things out, this challenge will die gradually.

2.1 How Unemployment has affected the Psychology of Nigerian Youths

The term psychology is the science of behaviour and mind, including conscious and unconscious phenomena, as well as feeling and thought. The menace of youth unemployment in

Nigeria has really affected how the youths see things within and outside the country. Their perception about the country is nothing good. Some of the youths because of their bad behaviour or perception towards the county have spent much money travelling to other African countries with the mindset that those countries are better than their own fatherland but at the end came back to their fatherland with nothing. Some of them began to build from scratch again just to meet up with the demand of life.

Have you ever engaged any Nigerian youth on what he thinks about the country? Have you ever asked him whether he still believes that something can still work out for good in the country? If you have not done that before, just try and carry out such kind of function one day.

Some Nigerian youths see Nigeria as a country that has failed. To them there is no amount of preaching you can give to them to change their belief. They have strong bitterness about the country where they are given birth. Some of them would tell you that nothing good can come out of the country again. One of the reasons for these negative thoughts is because of the unemployment and hardship in the country.

Also, there is serious moral decay in the country. So many Nigerian youths have left the good lives they were known with and are swimming in bad things because of what unemployment have put them into. So many believe that without tricks and cutting corners, that they will not make it in the country. They think differently in the negative direction and do things in the way they are not suppose to be done.

They do not believe in the government that control the affairs of the country. Everyone that occupies top leadership position in the country is seen as a coded criminal. They see every politician as the cause of their problem.

Another way through which unemployment has affected the Psychology of Nigerian youths is in the area of their attitude towards formal education. Some see going to the universities in

26

Nigeria as a waste of time. After spending 4 to 5 years in the university, there is no good job for them to fit in.

Some would say that it would have been better for them to learn the skill earlier than staying in the university for a long time and at the end no job opportunity. Youth unemployment has really changed the way young men and women in the country see things.

Because of the psychological effect of youth unemployment in Nigeria, some standard projects have been carried out by researchers. One of such researches is the one conducted by Omoniyi, Mary Banke Iyabo of Department of Guidance and Counselling, Faculty of Education Adekunle Ajasin University, Akungba Akoko, Ondo State, Nigeria. Part of the work states "The focus of this is to examine the psychological impacts of unemployment and underemployment on the mental health of Nigeria youths and the place of good governance and agricultural revolution as panacea. Research hypotheses were raised to guide the study. A self-constructed 25 item questionnaire was used to elicit information from the 167 subjects for the study". At the end of the research work, it was discovered that unemployment among the youths in Nigeria affects the mental health of the youths negatively.

This challenge gives sleepless nights to the undergraduate students studying in various universities in the country. Some of them feel severe headache due to this. Do you know why they feel such headache? It is not because they think more about the courses they study in their schools. But because they think of the burden they may bear after their graduation. It is called the burden of youth unemployment in Nigeria.

When they tune television sets to listen to news through some channels, one of the news that usually "seat" on top of the pages is the challenge of unemployment which hit the youths the most. Some of them began to ask themselves if they could really survive in the country. This sometimes affects the psychology of the young students as it shows in their attitudes towards their studies. Some of them would tell you that there is no need for them to kill themselves over their courses of study as those who have graduated from the universities are not doing any work.

The attitude of this kind gradually transforms them to see their studies in the schools as nothing. With time, some of them start missing lectures, make poor grades in the courses they suppose to have distinctions because of this challenge. Their thoughts, ideas and perceptions are negative because to them, there is no need to work hard academically as the hope of their survival after graduation is low. Their psychologies have been tampered with because of unemployment in the country. That is very bad in the country referred to as the giant of Africa continent.

There are so many youths that are insane in the country today. The insanity of some of these youths is severe. Many of those young people that find themselves in such state may be due to the frustration of unemployment in the country. They might have indulged in fetish activities to make money as they could not find any job that would pay them. This diabolic act sometimes backfires and ended up affecting the youths.

Some in that state do not understand what goes on in the environment they live. If proper research is carried out, you may find out that some of those mad youths are in that state because of frustration in life which one of them is youth unemployment.

2.2 Impact of Youth Unemployment on Nigeria economic Growth

Youth unemployment in Nigeria has really affected the economic growth of the Federal Republic of Nigeria negatively. There have been reports from media and elites on the danger of this national menace. The youths of this country are filled with strength and great capacities. When these capacities are not utilized properly, the economy of the country becomes affected.

The term unemployment could be used in relation to any of the factors of production which is idle and not being utilized properly for production. However, with reference to labour, there is unemployment if it is not possible to find jobs for all those who are eligible and able to work. Labour is said to be underemployed if it is working below capacity or not fully utilized in production (Anyawuocha, 1993).

Nigeria as a country has a fertile land for growing of crops. There is nothing you plant on the land that will not grow and give sound produce. The land of the country is blessed. But because of poor utility of the labour, this advantage is not utilized. The labours which in this context are the youths are underemployed.

Can you imagine what the economy of Nigeria will be like if the youths are employed and empowered in this sector to promote it? Within few years, the sector will blossom and there will be abundance of food in the country which will go a long way to promote the country's economy.

The impact of youth unemployment has really affected the economy of Nigeria negatively. Money is motivation. Incentives and support are motivation as well. Irrespective of the fact that some Nigerian youths may not like to go into agriculture, when they are motivated, they can do that. Creation of good enabling platform can propel them to practice agriculture and do it well.

When the government empower these young men and women by going into partnership with companies that will supply the necessary machines that will make the work easier for them, they will go into farming. There are many youths that are doing well in agriculture today. Some are in the east, others in the north, west, and southern parts of Nigeria. Many can do much better when motivated to practice it.

Youth agricultural unemployment has really reduced the country's strength in exportation of agricultural products. During the 1980s when youths were involved strongly in agriculture, the country exports many agricultural produce. The country was known globally for that. It boosted the economy of the country. But since the focus has been on crude oil, agriculture is abandoned. A slight decrease in the price of crude oil affects the economy of the country negatively. But if the youths are empowered and employed in the agricultural sector, any slight change in the price of oil will not affect the economy much.

The higher the youth unemployment, the lower the productivity rate of the country. There is higher disparity when 5 labourers are handling the production sector of a community in the country than when 12 sound persons are handling the same production in the same community. When there are more hands, more agricultural machines can be bought which in turn increases manufactured products. The increase in the number of labour as used implies employing of more youths as in this context.

When there is youth unemployment, the production rate becomes low. That is to say that less particular goods will be sold in the market places all over the country. In this scenario, the country will not generate much income. When the country does not make good profit, there is less money in circulation and the people suffer.

According to Legit, due to the increasing unemployment rate in Nigeria, there have been adverse effects on both the economy and the society. The consequences of unemployment in Nigeria includes: reduction in the national output of goods and services, increased rural-urban migration (Legit 2017).

Also, according to Ezie (2012), the unemployment situation in Nigeria is disturbing and even more disheartening that the country's economic condition cannot absorb an optimal proportion of its labour force. The words from Ezie still apply to youth unemployment in the country as well. From his view, because of high unemployment in the country less labour force is absorbed and due to that there is no optimum productivity.

Some companies will not like to invest in a country which has unemployment issue in a high rate. The fact is that unemployment is synonymous to poverty. When companies take statistics of what unemployment is doing to a particular society, they may be disturbed internally of the risk of running their businesses in such community. A lot of negative questions come into their minds. These make them to back off instead of coming into the country to invest to make profits and grow the economy of the country.

Unemployment has done so much harm to the country. Investors are afraid to come into the country to invest. The fear of the unknown has kept them far from coming close to the country. Their coming in can boost the economy of the country but the challenge of youth unemployment has kept them far from reaching the country. The country's economy is staggering because the right investors are not attracted. The government want them to invest but many of them are afraid because of the bad state of the country.

Instead of the investors to come into the country to invest, they move over to countries which the economies are better and the youths already utilizing their energy for the betterment of their societies. They do this because they believe that the youths will have industrial experiences already and can fit into their jobs as quickly as possible. Unlike in Nigeria, the investors may spend huge amount of money training the youth to acquire the necessary skills before they fit into the jobs they are employed to do.

2.3 Causes of Youth Unemployment in Nigeria

Any country that has high unemployment rate in the world has its causes. It is either the fault of the individuals that make up the country or the leaders of the country. In the case of the Federal Republic of Nigeria, the average citizens of the country point at the government as the cause of the problem. But in the real sense, the government of Nigeria alone is not just the cause of youth employment. Sometimes there are some factors that cause this challenge of youth unemployment that are not just the fault of the government alone.

In this section, to be discussed are the causes of youth unemployment in Nigeria. These are strong points that can be used for academic or any other purposes. The causes of youth unemployment in Nigeria are as follow:

- Inadequate skill development by the youths

- Poor planning

- Tribalism and nepotism

- High dependence on imported products

- Inability to see beyond theoretical study

- Poor supply of electricity

- Corruption

- Poor exploitation of mineral resources

- None creativity of the government

- Selfishness of Nigerian leaders

- Unemployable skills

- Poor mentorship

- Bad economy

- Poor personal and leadership development

- Over population

Poor supply of electricity

Electricity is the major driver in the production processes of many developed countries in the world. Since the discovery of electricity, man has been able to make more progress in terms of economy. Any country that does not have the adequate power supply lacks behind in global economic performance.

For the average Nigerian youth that wants to venture into entrepreneurship, constant source of power supply is essential for most businesses (Olawale 2018). The impact made in most small and medium businesses is most times directly proportional to strength of electricity supply. When the power supply is poor, the business will struggle and suffer.

Take for instance that a youth graduated from the university. After his graduation, he found out that he is able to save small amount of money when he was in the university. With this money, he purchased about six computers to start Cyber Café business. He felt strong at the beginning of the business.

But after running the business for six months, he found out that he spent most of the gain he made from the business in buying of petrol to run the café due to the power challenge in the country. He may grow cold feet as this continues. This may make him to quit and join the unemployed youths as he is discouraged with the situation. The gain the youth makes is supposed to be invested into the business for expansion of the business but inadequate electricity supply makes it impossible.

Inability to see beyond theoretical study

It takes wisdom for a student to start searching for the black goat before the day becomes dark. The reason behind it is that once the day is dark, the goat becomes same colour with the night. This will make the person in search of the black goat to find it difficult to discover where the black goat may be in the absence of light.

Those sentences have great wisdom in them. Little number of Nigerian youths only think outside the box when they were in the institutions of higher learning. This makes them to find it difficult to get employed after graduation. It is not all about theories. Most theoretical teachings in the universities sometimes have no sound applications in the real life when the students do not go extra mile.

HTML for example is a computer language learnt in computer science course. HTML is a programming language and it stands for Hypertext Markup Language. Some youths just memorize how to write this language without thinking on how to apply what they learn to be self employed and make money for themselves even when they were still in school.

Some intelligent youths who learnt this language have already started building and designing websites for clients before their graduation. But for some who just learnt the theory because they wanted to write the exams and make good grades, ended up being unemployed after they leave school. Inability to see beyond theoretical study among Nigerian youths has added to high unemployment rate.

Tribalism and nepotism

Who do you know in Nigeria? How strong is your connection? Do you have strong connection? They are common questions job seekers contemplate on when they find themselves in the circle of employment.

Quoting the words of Alex on nepotism, he stated, "Nepotism has been singled out as a major problem facing unemployed youths in sub-Saharan Africa. This was revealed last week in Kigali at a conference organised by Africa Economic Research Consortium.

The conference noted that youths with no political connections hardly secure employment compared with those from families with political background". It is a fact and that is the reason why the poor are getting poorer and the rich getting richer. It has disqualified many youths from having good jobs to do.

Because some Nigerian youths that secure jobs obtained the jobs either by who they know or because the person occupying the top position is from their tribe, maximum results are not achieved. If you are an expert in a particular field and your level of experience would have made a company make more money and expand to other branches, and instead of hiring you, another person who has

41

less experience is hired because he is politically connected, the produce to be generated will be low.

Behaviour of this kind will make profit generated to be low and hence no expansion. The expansion would have resulted to more job creation for the youths but tribalism and nepotism has hindered such opportunity. Political connections feature prominently in almost all regions of Africa.

High dependence on imported products

There are some imported goods that can be made in Nigeria. The citizens of this country including the youths can make these products which are imported from Europe and other countries. Dependence on those products made in abroad has made youth unemployment in the country high.

In the recent year, the government of the Federal Republic of Nigeria banned the importation of foreign rice into the country. Though many Nigerians frowned at the policy made by the country's head but such policy has given some jobs to the youths that have gone into agriculture.

High dependence of the country on already made goods from other countries end up promoting the economy of those countries and in return brings about increase in youth unemployment. The perception of an average Nigerian is that goods made in foreign countries are superior to those made here in Nigeria. But that is wrong. If standard raw materials are supplied, standard products of such kind can be made in Nigeria as well.

Businessmen and women in the country do not want restrictions on importation of certain goods because they are making profit through importation. But that is not good as it causes more harm than good to the youths and the entire nation. When the businessmen and women made their money, they use it to enrich themselves and families but when the productions are carried out in the country, more people benefit because of job creation and boost of the economy of the country.

Corruption

Corruption is the dishonest or fraudulent conduct by those in power, typically involving bribery. It is the illegitimate use of power to benefit a private interest (Morris 1991). Corruption practices mean the offering, giving, receiving, or soliciting, directly or indirectly, of anything of value to influence the action of the public official in the procurement process or in contract execution (Farida Waziri 2010).

In the year 2000, Transparency International carried out a survey on the corruption level of 90 countries, including Kenya, Cameroon, Angola, Nigeria, Côte-d'Ivoire, Zimbabwe, Ethiopia, Ghana, Senegal, Zambia, India, Venezuela, Moldova, and others. At the end of the ranking, Nigeria was seen as the most corrupt in that ranking because the country occupied the 90th position in terms of transparency. Nigeria was the most corrupt country in the year 2000. Though the result has improved in the recent time but corruption still shows its red head in many public sectors in the country.

As of October 04, 2018, the phrase "corruption in Nigeria" generates over 58. 7 million searches related topics on Google search engine. That is evidence that corruption in the Federal Republic of Nigeria is a hot topic. It is a menace that has stayed in the country for a very long time. It is disappointing that corruption is a disease that has no cure yet in the country.

Nigeria has rank low in terms of transparency due to the fact that the country has dirty record. Denmark is one of the countries that records low corruption level and the challenge of unemployment is not much when compared with Nigeria. They balance things up because they want to make progress in their country. Countries that rank high in corruption hardly progress in their dealings.

Corruption in Nigeria is one of the major causes of youth unemployment. How can the youths secure good jobs when the leaders of the country are embezzling the funds that are to be used for the development of the society? The annoying thing is not that these wicked leaders stole the public funds but they went and dump the money in foreign banks. These banks use the money to develop their own country.

If not because of their shallow thinking, they would have used the money to raise production and other companies which in turn will give jobs to the youths. But in all, corruption is bad. It keeps a country dormant. If everyone because of the opportunity they have to be at the top keep embezzling the funds that are made for public use for their own personal use, things will not go well in the country.

When funds are apportioned to build infrastructure to facilitate job creation in the society and the head of the team spends some and pockets some, it becomes an issue. There will be no full completion of the project. In that regards, an avenue that suppose to create jobs for the youths are made dormant. Corruption is one of the causes of many abandoned government projects observed all over Nigeria.

Inadequate skill development by the youths

Skill is a very important tool that any youth that wants to live enjoyable life in any society needs to acquire. It is as a result of inadequate skill acquisition by the youths of the country that makes some of the youths to be unemployed. No company that wants to make progress in their business will employ any youth that does not have good skill.

When a youth is not skilful in one way or the other, he becomes a burden to the company that may employ him. And because no company will like to employ an individual that will be a burden to them, they end up not employing such youth and at all. And when this is experienced, the numbers of unemployed youths in the country keep increasing.

Skill acquisition irrespective of how small it may be is one of the ways a youth can empower his or herself. When a youth have a skill in a particular field, he or she can be self employed. But when this is lacking, the youth becomes a liability.

Poor skill acquisition has made some Nigerian youths fail during interviews as job seekers. When the interviewers ask "what can you do? ". Many are thrown off balance because they have no tangible skills. Many are just dependent on what they were taught in the school. They fail to give the interviewers answers on what they can do. Because of this, their numbers add to those who are not employed. Poor skill acquisition is like a person that wants to grow crops but he does not know how to farm.

Poor planning

The saying "failure to plan is planning to fail" is real and practical. When you decided not to plan your life properly, expect failure. In the same way, if you as a youth do not take good steps on how to make your life better, expect failure which when applied in respect to this topic is unemployment. Poor planning among Nigerian youths is one of the fundamental causes of youth unemployment in Nigeria.

If you fully understand the nature of the country where you find yourself, you have to make adequate plan on how to win. When you are ignorant on how to win by not planning ahead of time, you will find yourself in the circle of people being affected by this youth challenge. But when you make some plans on time, you will not be trapped.

There are some youths whom before they graduated from their institutions of higher learning have already started making money. They were making the small token from the part-time jobs they do. With the jobs they do even as undergraduates, they build themselves. They start making plans on how to develop fully in that field when they graduate.

Some of them immediately after their graduation, they build strongly that which they made plan to expand. Ideas are very important for proper self development. Not having the ideas to plan towards the real life as a youth still in school have shamefully added to the number of unemployed youths in Nigeria.

Some youths that want to go into business did not plan on time.

They do not plan properly on the kind of environment such business will excel. The best or the kinds of products that will sell most are not considered. Also, the audience to target for maximum results were not put into plan. As a result of this, many go into businesses and fell out after some time. They lost a lot of capital and time because of improper plan. In the long run, the business folds up and they could not continue. When this happens, they become unemployed again and add to the number of unemployed youths nationwide.

Selfishness of the Nigerian leaders

Show me those leaders who are not selfish and I will show you a society that has low youth unemployment rate. That is a fact. When the leaders of a country are selfish, they think only of themselves and not what will favour the entire citizens of the country. Their selfishness creates high youth unemployment rate in the country.

How can the law makers in the country be so selfish to make a policy that pays each of them an annual pay of over two million US dollars (over $2,000 000)? Is that not selfishness and wickedness? They make some laws to their favour and then share the country's resources among themselves because they are the people that made the laws.

Nigerian senators as well as other leaders of the country are selfish and shallow minded. They do not think far. How can the monthly salary of a Nigerian senator be much higher than that of the senator of the United States of America? In terms of achievements and other positive developments needed in every country, United States is far better than Nigeria and yet the senators in the country pay themselves far more than those of the United States.

The Nigerian media has long reported that Nigerian parliamentarians are the most highly paid in the world. Comparison with compensation paid to U.S. senators and representatives might be instructive. U.S. senator or representative earns a salary of $174,000 per year (John Campbell 2018).

Upon the money paid to the US senators when compared to that of Nigerian senators, US senators still have more works to do than the Nigerians. In 2010, one estimate was that an average senator received $3.3 million in allowances to cover staff salaries, office space, postage, and myriad other expenses (ibid).

Of a truth, selfishness of the leaders of the Federal Republic of Nigeria has resulted to high youth unemployment in the country. Why not cut the money paid to these senators, members of House of Representatives, and governors and use the money to create more jobs for the youths? The challenge will continue if they do not change their attitudes. It is sad and unaccountable for people who pretend to be caring for the ones they lead to be robbing them.

Because of their selfishness, the country suffers. The youths suffer. No good infrastructural development to help the young ones get jobs and start earning their living. The earning disparity between politicians and civil servants is so much. If they do not want to tell themselves the truth and address this issue, youth unemployment in the country will continue to be on the rise.

Bad Economy

This is a strong point in the current time in the Federal Republic of Nigeria. The economic condition of Nigeria had been weak in the recent time. This has affected many businesses in the country and many have shutdown.

In the year 2016, Nigeria got into recession and the effect of the challenge is still felt in the country today. So many youths lost their jobs when this happened and added to the rise in the statistics. Some companies could not pay their workers any longer and had to close down.

The major cause of the economic recession then was the drop in the crude oil price which happens to be the major source of income to the country. This incidence was published by BBC news report. The company through her news reported thus in 2016: "Nigeria has slipped into recession, with the latest growth figures showing the economy contracted 2.06% between April and June.

The country has now seen two consecutive quarters of declining growth, the usual definition of recession. Its vital oil industry has been hit by weaker global prices, according to the Nigerian Bureau of Statistics (NBS). But the government says there has been strong growth in other sectors.

Crude oil sales account for 70% of government income. The price of oil has fallen from highs of about $112 a barrel in 2014 to below $50 at the moment. Outside the oil industry, the figures show the fall in the Nigerian currency, the naira, has hurt the economy. It was allowed to float freely in June to help kick-start the economy, but critics argued it should have been done earlier" (BBC 2016).

None Creativity of the Nigerian Government

Because the government of Nigeria is not creative enough in their dealing, they fail to create enough jobs for the youths of the country. They do not brainstorm properly to device means to tackle pressing needs of the people. Creativity is the use of imagination or original ideas to create something; inventiveness. In this context, creativity is the ability of the Nigerian government to use their ideas to create jobs for large number of the country's youths.

The government of the country is lacking in this area. A government that have been exporting the crude oil produced in her country to another country for refining for years without building their own refineries since those years are not creative. How much will it take the government to build such refineries in the country to create jobs and at the same time boost the economy of the country?

Speaking at the 5th Triennial National Delegates Conference of the Petroleum and Natural Gas Senior Staff Association of Nigeria, PENGASSAN in Abuja Kachikwu described as embarrassing the country's inability to refine oil in the country (Adekunle 2017). That was the voice of Ibe Kachikwu on the issue that the Nigerian government has not been able to build their own refineries. Emmanuel Ibe Kachikwu is the Minister of State, Petroleum Resources currently and the immediate past Group Managing

Director, Nigerian National Petroleum Corporation (August 2015 –

4-June 2016).

The Minister said that Nigeria should be able to produce enough petroleum products to meet domestic needs, and stressed that changing times in the industry suggested that the country must look for ways of ensuring efficient management of the refineries and make them productive or lose them and the job opportunities it offers. From the further view of Kachikwu which is not far from the view this book looks at, building our own refineries will create reasonable employment opportunities for Nigerians as well as the youths.

A government that is creative will not have one source as the major means through which the country makes money to build their capital. That is weak and shallow. The country is blessed with so many mineral resources. If the government is creative enough, they suppose to have called some experts to find solid applications of these mineral resources. This will be another good source of income to the country. But a situation where they do not reason toward this direction, the small available space becomes a tug of war as many are fighting to fit in into the small available opportunity.

Nigeria is one of those countries in Africa that has a wide variety of different natural resources. These minerals are not properly exploited. If these are to be in Europe, they would have gained much from them. But because of the bad leadership, they are not put   in   use. Nigeria is richly endowed with a variety of natural resources ranging from precious metals various stones to industrial value such as Barites, Gypsum, Kaolin and Marble. Most of these are yet to be exploited. Statistically, the level of exploitation of these minerals is very low in relation to the extent of deposit found in the country. One of the objectives of the new National Policy on Solid Minerals is to ensure the orderly development of the mineral resources of the country (Federal Ministry of Youth and Sports Development 2018). The minerals which the country is blessed with are much.

The table below shows individual areas in Nigeria with unique mineral resources. Take a look and see what or government can work with to create good job opportunities for the Nigerian youths.

S/N	STATES	NATURAL RESOURCES
1	Abia	Gold, Lead/Zinc, Limestone, Oil/Gas & Salt
2	Abuja	Cassiterite, Clay, Dolomite, Gold, Lead/Zinc, Marble & Tantalite
3	Adamawa	Bentonite, Gypsium, Kaolin & Magnesite
4	Akwa Ibom	Clay, Lead/Zinc, Lignite, Limestone, Oil/Gas, Salt & Uranium
5	Anambra	Clay, Glass-Sand, Gypsium, Iron-ore, Lead/Zinc, Lignite, Limestone, Phosphate & Salt
6	Bauchi	Gold, Cassiterite (tine ore), Columbite, Gypsium, Wolfram, Coal, Limestone, Lignite, Iron-ore & Clay
7	Bayelsa	Glay, Gypsium, Lead/Zinc, Lignite, Limestone, Maganese, Oil/Gas & Uranium
8	Benue	Barite, Clay, Coal, Gemstone, Gypsium, Iron-Ore, Lead/Zinc, Limestone, Marble & Salt
9	Borno	Bentonite, Clay, Diatomite, Gypsium, Hydro-carbon,

		Kaolin & Limestone
10	Cross River	Barite, Lead/Zinc, Lignite, Limestone, Manganese, Oil/Gas, Salt & Uranium
11	Delta	Clay, Glass-sand, Gypsium, Iron-ore, Kaolin, Lignite, Marble & Oil/Gas
12	Ebonyi	Gold, Lead/Zinc & Salt
13	Edo	Bitumen, Clay Dolomite, Phosphate, Glass-sand, Gold, Gypsium, Iron-ore, Lignite, Limestone, Marble & Oil/Gas
14	Ekiti	Feldspar, Granite, Kaolin, Syenite & Tatium
15	Enugu	Coal, Lead/Zinc & Limestone
16	Gombe	Gemstone & Gypsium
17	Imo	Gypsium, Lead/Zinc, Lignite, Limestone, Marcasite, Oil/Gas, Phosphate & Salt
18	Jigawa	Butyles
19	Kaduna	Amethyst, Aqua Marine, Asbestos, Clay, Flosper, Gemstone, Gold, Graphite, Kaolin, Hyanite, Mica, Rock Crystal, Ruby, Sapphire, Sihnite, Superntinite, Tentalime, Topaz & Tourmaline
20	Kano	Gassiterite, Copper, Gemstone, Glass-sand, Lead/Zinc, Pyrochinre & Tantalite
21	Katsina	Kaolin, Marble & Salt

22	Kebbi	Gold
23	Kogi	Cole, Dolomite, Feldspar, Gypsium, Iron-ore, Kaolin, Marble, Talc & Tantalite
24	Kwara	Cassiterite, Columbite, Feldspar, Gold, Iron-ore, Marble, Mica & Tantalite
25	Lagos	Bitumen, Clay & Glass-sand
26	Nasarawa	Amethyst (Topaz Garnet), Barytex, Barite, Cassirite, Chalcopyrite, Clay, Columbite, Coking Coal, Dolomite/Marble, Feldspar, Galena, Iron-ore, Limstone, Mica, Salt, Sapphire, Talc, Tantalite, Tourmaline Quartz & Zireon
27	Niger	Gold, Lead/Zinc & Talc
28	Ogun	Bitumen, Clay, Feldspar, Gemstone, Kaolin, Limestone & Phosphate
29	Ondo	Bitumen, Clay, Coal, Dimension Stones, Feldspar, Gemstone, Glass-Sand, Granite, Gypsium, Kaolin, Limestone & Oil/Gas
30	Osun	Columbite, Gold, Granite, Talc, Tantalite & Tourmaline
31	Oyo	Aqua Marine, Cassiterite, Clay, Dolomite, Gemstone,

		Gold, Kaolin, Marble, Silimonite, Talc & Tantalite
32	Plateau	Barite, Bauxite, Betonite, Bismuth, Cassiterite, Clay, Coal, Emeral, Fluoride, Gemstone, Granite, Iron-ore, Kaolin, Lead/Zinc, Marble, Molybdenite, Phrochlore, Salt, Tantalite/Columbite, Tin & Wolfram
33	Rivers	Clay, Glass-Sand, Lignite, Marble & Oil/Gas
34	Sokoto	Clay, Flakes, Gold, Granite, Gypsium, Kaolin, Laterite, Limestone, Phosphate, Potash, Silica Sand & Salt
35	Taraba	Lead/Zinc
36	Yobe	Soda Ash & Tintomite
37	Zamfara	Coal, Cotton & Gold

Fig 2.1: Mineral resources/ raw materials in different parts of Nigeria; Source: Federal Ministry of Youth and Sports Development.

Inviting both local and international investors for the exploitation of these mineral resources will be a plus to the country. The value the exploitation of these minerals will add to the country will be imaginable. Because the government in terms of creativity is poor, she is not able to establish a reasonable link to make this work out. They are all concentrating their attentions strongly on crude oil. What it implies is that the country is finished if anything happens to the crude oil of the country. The wise run to hide before it starts raining heavily.

They forgot that building their trust mainly on the oil is like someone that has all his eggs in one basket. If anything happens to the basket that will be the end of everything. A standard creative government will not do such thing. Since the government of the country fail to be creative in utilizing the resources to create more jobs for the youths, there rise in unemployment rate in the country becomes a normal thing. It is like a culture and nobody is moved again concerning the challenge of youth unemployment in the country.

Poor mentorship

In developed countries of the world, the importance of mentorship is solidly observed. They really understand the value a mentor can add to the lives of young people in their society. But here in Nigeria, it is not taken any serious. Any young person that is not directed by the more experienced one in the society is likely to make some mistakes in his or her life.

What is mentorship and who is a mentor? Mentorship is a relationship in which a more experienced or more knowledgeable person helps to guide a less experienced or less knowledgeable person. The mentor may be older or younger than the person being mentored, but he or she must have a certain area of expertise. Nigerian youths can choose their mentors. This will help them to make the right choice as they move ahead in life.

In Europe, young people have their mentors even before they gained admission into institutions of higher learning. Their mentors guide them on what life is about and then the tricks they need to apply to win in life struggle. The good thing is that when these young people are properly established through the knowledge they gain from their mentors, they can go higher in life.

It does not just end there. There are even schools in Europe and North America where the young pay before they receive rich advice from their mentors. Some of the mentees that had mentors are great persons in their individual societies today. They are great because they acquired important skills and nutritional information from their mentors.

In the area of mentorship, the mentor must not be older than the person being mentored. In Nigeria universities, some youths may meet people who are well experienced than them in a particular area they have passion in, but because of age factor, they fail to make such persons their mentors. That is a wrong ideology many Nigerian youths have and it is robbing them from many things they might have learnt in life. So many youths who found excellent jobs they are doing today is because they had good mentors that make them more knowledgeable in a the area they had passion for.

Employable skills needed by the youths can be acquired through mentorship. But a situation where Nigerian youths do not want to tap into this benefit, they end up not have any tangible skill. This in turn makes them unemployed. The statistics of unemployed youths is high in the country because they fail to have at least a mentor/coach that will put them through in certain things about life. Note that the author of this book got into writing and other technical skills because he was mentored by a younger mentor whose name is **Late Igili Onyedikachukwu**.

Poor personal and leadership development

Personal development is experienced when a person decides to use the available tool he has to cause a positive change. It is not just change but a positive change. The available tool here can be the person's ideas, money or land. When he properly uses them, he will have good result and be happy at the end. Successful people maintained and achieved successful standard because they were able to use the tools they have to cause positive change.

Nigerian youths need self development to achieve excellence and at the same time useful in the society. There are many ideas in our

65

youths. The challenge is that some of them do not want to try their hands. Some are afraid that they may not excel in those ideas which they have to move themselves forward. Why not try those ideas first? Ideas rule the world.

In the world of writing, there are many that are great authors today but do you know where they started? They started as simple students that wrote essays of about 500 words. From such essays they began to write longer ones of about 700 words each. As time continued, they began to write articles of about 1,500 words.

Some of these writers who started as mere essay writers at a point got ideas on how they will expand their articles for the larger persons to read them. After some researches based on the ideas decided to build blog websites where the masses can land and write read their articles. Like joke, some are rich in the society today because they advertise for companies on their blog sites who pay them in return.

On the other hand, some of these people who started as ordinary essay writers before they discovered themselves have some books that are selling globally on Amazon and through some other channel. Before they started writing standard books, they got the ideas and at the end made them real. Their books sell every month and they make money from them. These are previous essay writers that latter discovered themselves. Youth unemployment in Nigeria still persists because many Nigeria youths do not make effort to discover what ideas that will make them win their unemployed status.

Mark Zuckerberg (founder of Facebook) is successful today because he was able to use his available tool to cause positive change for himself. In his case, his tool is great ideas and computer programming skills. He designed a platform that will bring students together to share ideas and hence the name Facebook. The programming skill and ideas he has transformed into great success as he did not only bring world students together on his platform but the entire world. Today, Mark is respected as the world richest youth because he was able utilize his tool.

Nigeria can eradicate youth unemployment if they follow the footstep of the Facebook owner. One of the reasons for the high youth unemployment rate is because we have not start using the tools we have. Our own tools here are the mineral resources we have. They are much and can give huge return if properly exploited. Poor exploitation of the resources given to the country by nature is the reason for our backwardness.

 It is not an abomination if the government of the country makes a policy that will mandate the rich citizens of the country to invest massively into the exploitation of these natural resources. If there are five rich people doing that in each state, it will go a long way to utilize the materials that we have laying fresh. With time, Nigeria will start producing things they were not producing before. These products can be exported to other countries and with time build strong income for the country.

There are so many manufacturing companies that will be glad to come in and assist in the exploitation of these raw materials. Youth unemployment still persists because the government have not taken their time to send delegates to these companies for their partnership. Irrespective of the fact that the country produces engineers every year, where are these engineers working today?

Some of them do not have any job and some find themselves in the banking sector. They find themselves in those states because there is no exploitation of the raw materials available in the country. Crude oil is not the only raw material the country has. There are still many others. When these materials are exploited to some extent, they will find somewhere they will fit in. This will make them happy and fulfilled. But when the proper utility of these material are not put into consideration by both the government and the capable citizens of the country, we will continue to find ourselves in this mess called youth unemployment.

Unemployable skills

A youth without an employable skill is like a beautiful lady without a good character. She looks very attractive in the eyes but when you go closer to her, you will be shocked to find out that her behaviour smells so bad like rotten egg. And nobody will be happy to have rotten egg besides him irrespective of how good the egg may look at the outside.

That young man is cute. He looks so handsome. See how he looks so smart in his dressing. Relax, it is not all about that. Does he have the needed employable skill? Can he work effectively for us to get the results we want to attain in our company? That is what is more important and not about how he looks.

Show me that youth that possesses certain employable skill and I will show you that youth that cannot be unemployed. In fact, show him to me and I will show you a youth that many companies are ready to pay huge just for them to have him. What can Nigerian youths do? If you are a Nigerian youth that can do something good skilfully, then you are employable. Unemployment is not for you.

The reason why some Nigerian youths are not employed is because of the fact that they do not posses certain employable skills. Those who have employable skills even if they do not have companies that will employ them can employ themselves. That is called self employment.

For many years running, most Nigerian youths have disdained acquisition of skill, thinking that time spent on such is a waste, and opting for the so-called white 'clean and easy ways of making money. With such mentality, these youths have grown into middle-age and even senior age without any skill to show, thus becoming liability to themselves and others.

Recently, irrespective of the fact that some youths have Bachelor's degrees, they still learn some other skills to back up the certificate they acquired from the universities. Some of them are into tailoring while others are into makeup. The reason behind those extra steps they took is to acquire skills and make themselves employable.

In the same view, some of them who studied metallurgical and materials engineering after their university went into welding to learn welding skills. In the course of their learning, they are added among the number of unemployed youths in the country. Some after learning establish themselves based on what they learned and some others find jobs in other companies (Nigerian Finder 2015).

Overpopulation

According to Maduawuchi, our population increases without a proportional increase in the avenues of employment opportunities thereby leaving a large proportion of the population unemployed (Maduawuchi 2017). In some communities in Nigeria, people believe that God is the giver of children and therefore will continue to give birth to babies without any form of control. To such people, there is nothing like birth control or family planning. Such practice is not in their dictionary or plan at all.

This is one of the reasons for the increase in the rate of unemployment in the country. Those who do not consider family planning as an option do not think deep on the issue of unemployment in the country. Their own is to give birth to children and multiply.

The attitude of giving birth to many children without control have robbed our youths opportunity to get jobs from the limited available ones. Many persons are struggling to fit in to the little available space. When the available space is fully occupied, the remaining are left unemployed.

Because of the high number of the Nigerian youths on the streets which are so much because many of the parents do not practice family planning, some of the young girls are into prostitution. They have taken prostitution as their full-time job because they need to meet up. The annoying thing is that those that brought them into the world do not know some of them again because they are much.

Some of them in the course of their hustle to make money through prostitution fail into the hands of wicked ritualists and their lives end there. This is bad as it place the young ladies in our land on red light. It is a risky engagement and it does not tell well of the persons. But they are into this shit for their survival.

In the northern Nigeria, the issue of overpopulation is high.

Because of illiteracy and religious belief, people give birth without control. A man over there can have 7 wives with over 30 children. When these children grow into youths, they struggle to secure jobs with the slim available employment opportunities. Some of them may not get and hence add to the number of the unemployed youths in the country. Also, the reason why northerners are overpopulated is political. They want to have higher headcounts to win political positions.

Due to their poor thinking, they derive joy in having large number of children so that they can vote in their own person into political positions. Northerners in Nigeria have the highest population in the country. They use this higher population as advantage over other ethnic groups. Any candidate contesting for a particular political position, like the position of the presidency in the country hardly fails when he has the support and the votes of the northerners.

2.4 Effects of Youth Unemployment in Nigeria

The young men and women in the country want to survive. They

74

are filled with strengths and if these their strengths are not controlled when they are facing the unemployment issue, they can be channelled wrongly. The effects of youth unemployment in Nigeria are as follow:

- Advancement in crime

- Frustration

- Increase in Poverty rate

- Migration

- Unpatriotic and disloyalty

- Increase in the number of dependent people

Advancement in Crime

The rise in criminal activities in Nigeria has strong origin. So many vices in the country which Nigerian youths are fully involved have some of them as a result of youth unemployment. Some of them when they seek for jobs and do not get picks criminal activities as option for survival.

Delta state governor, Dr Emmanuel Uduaghan has attributed the

75

spate of terrorism and other violent crimes in the country including

kidnapping largely to the problem of youth unemployment, which

he said, had been neglected over the years (Austin Ogwuda 2014).

He further stated that the problem might not be solved overnight

because lack of employment over the years created a pool of

youths who are being recruited for insurgency and other nefarious

activities. It is sad to see our youths whom are to be building the

country destroying it.

The highest kidnapping activities in the country are carried out by

the youths of the country. Some of them are doing that not because

they like it but because they want to survive. In few cases, they

have targeted Nigerian politicians because they believe they are

one of the root causes of unemployment in Nigeria which is why

they find themselves in the dirty business they do.

An armed robber that steals on the street knows that it is very risky

because he may get caught or shot down at a spot during operation.

But most of them are careless about that because they are ready to die. To some of them, it is either they succeed through the dirty business of armed robbery or die. Death is nothing to them because "all die na die" (meaning that all death are death).

Unemployment among young men and women in Nigeria has pushed some of them into robbery. A Nigerian graduate once confessed that why he was into robbery was due to unemployment. Oluwasegun made this confession when he was caught during robbery operation.

He stated during the interrogation by a police officer, "*I am a 2012 graduate of Mechanical Engineering from the University of Port Harcourt, Rivers State. I did my youth service in Delta State At the moment, I am unemployed*". Some of them rob on streets without fear after taking hard drugs that made them high and do things that they may not ordinarily do. Communities do not sleep with their two eyes well closed because of what the challenge of unemployment has pushed our young people into.

Some have crossed their minds to the extent that they see human lives as nothing. "Your money or your life" is one of the slogans they use during their activities. Some sometimes kill their victims through gun shots even when they have acquired what they wanted during robbery. They feel so bitter deep down in their hearts because of what poor organization of the country has turned them into.

The modern scammers in the country still want to make head ways in their criminal activities. Some of these young men and women after waiting for a long time and did not find any job that would pay them well decided to go into internet and other forms of scams. It is not good as these young people of the Federal Republic of Nigeria are seriously advancing in this criminal act.

Every day, social media accounts of users are hacked by these criminals. They are called Yahoo or G boys. These are the young men that are into scam mainly internet scam in the country. The trending is the Yahoo or G girls. These are the upcoming youths who are into the same scam but are the female gender.

It is hard to go into cities in the country without seeing these young men and women driving big and expensive cars on the street. They are the big guys and ladies that have made it on the street as many use it. They do street according to the common slang used by them. You hear something like this, "do you know that guy has made it through street?"

The pitiable situation is that even some parents are happy to see their children as they make money through internet scam. Based on personal experience, in a city of Abraka, in Ethiope East local government area of Delta state, there are many youths who are G boys. In this town, internet scam is observed as culture. People see it as normal and nothing bad. The scammers drive cars round the city and kill people through accidents.

Some of them have gone diabolic because they want to make it big. They use the devilish powers to make their victims believe in everything they say. At the end, the victim sends the amount of money they asked for irrespective of the location the victim lives.

Some of these young scammers do not even consider the negative effects of what they do.

Because of high unemployment rate in the country, some youths have taken the scam as their full-time job. They can press their computers from morning to evening as they search for clients they will scam. They are intelligent but use their intelligence wrongly. The society is seriously decaying morally as a result of youth unemployment.

Frustration

You hear things like, "guy I feel like dying because am tired of this so country called"; "I do not know why God decided to bring me into this stupid country"; what is the essence of living in this country when nothing is working"; "I can't believe that this is me, after studying mechanical engineering for 5 years in the university, this is where I am doing nothing"; "My guy, Nigeria is fucked big time". These and many other complains you hear from Nigeria youths whom have been hit hard by the challenge of unemployment in the country.

It is not a child's play at all. A hungry youth is an angry youth. He needs food for his survival and when he is not finding any feels bitter and frustrated. Frankly, Nigerian youths are suffering and they are in great pains. So many of them are tired of complaining.

Their parents and guardians are waiting for their manifestations. They want to see those whom they spent much money on during their universities days manifest. They are patiently waiting for when they will start paying back for the money they spent on them by giving back to them when they start working. But they are not seeing any positive change.

The youths wake up in the morning asking themselves so many rhetorical questions concerning their lives. It is a big challenge. Many of them that do not have strong hearts ended up as dead persons due to frustrations in life. They see the time they spent in the universities as waste. Who will they complain to? They are getting tired of existing in the country called the giant of Africa.

As if the frustrations they pass through in their lives are not enough, the younger ones and relations are mounting pressure. The question they usually ask is "when are you going to start helping us with the dues we pay in schools?" Other relations will ask "when are you getting married?" We need to know this "our wife to be". These are the questions directed to someone who is hungry. Questions of these kind increases the pressure more. Young persons in Nigeria are passing through some situations they themselves sometimes find difficult to explain.

Increase in poverty rate

Poverty is a disease. It has hit Nigerian youths hard. The menace has kept not only the youths thinking but the entire citizens of Nigeria. Some have no food to eat. Some wake up in the morning just for them to be cracking their brains of what they would eat for the day. People have stolen in market places and are beaten to death for stealing because they were hungry. It is a common jungle justice found in many places in the country.

What is the definition of poverty? Poverty is defined as the lack of minimum food and shelter necessary for maintaining life. It can also be referred to as absolute poverty. When one earns less and lacks shelter to the extent that he or she cannot feed properly and meet up with the demand of life, the person is said to be poor. Further, it is the condition of lacking sufficient money or goods to meet basic human needs such as food, shelter and clothing.

Poverty gap at 1.25 dollar a day (PPP) (%) in Nigeria was measured at 33.74 in 2010, according to the World Bank. According to the same source, Poverty headcount ratio at dollar1.25 a day (PPP) (% of population) in Nigeria was measured at 67.98 in the same year 2010. According to the World Bank data, based on the Poverty headcount ratio at $1.90 per day, 53.5% of the country's population were unemployed in 2003. In the year 2009, the rate still stood at 53.5% base on the same standard (World Bank).

How can a youth that has no means of living feed properly? He most times relies on the help from friends and people around him. Some Nigerian youths get married late mainly because of their poor state. Unemployment in the country has turned them to be poor. It made them have poor self esteem.

Many youths in the country smell the poor state of the country all over themselves. This is why some have applied for visa on many occasions and did not get them and yet have not given up in applying the more. They want to leave the poor circle of the country. They are not happy any longer.

Youth unemployment produced youth poverty. Youths are made to be lively and sound but the unemployment state in the country has made the reverse be the case to some of them. They are lost and find it difficult to cope with their demanding activities. A poor youth is incapacitated to do greater things as a youth.

Underpayment of the youths that do manual works in the country is not new. When the rich hire these young men to do work for them, they are not paid as supposed. This is because they have no say.

They need money to feed and keep lives going. So, rather than rejecting the pay, they prefer to pick the small pay. Instead of the work they do to make them rich, it does not because they are not paid properly. This is because there is no availability of jobs. There is no job anywhere in the country. So, they have to pick the one they have irrespective of the poor pay.

Put simply, many people live in poverty because they are unable to find a job that pays a living wage—or to find a job at all (Teaching Tolerance 2012). To be sure, not everyone who is unemployed lives in poverty, but in this subheading you have "digested" looked at how unemployment and underemployment often contribute to poverty among Nigerian youths. It is an issue that needs to be addressed by every city of the country.

Migration

Young men and women in Nigeria would not choose the country if they are given the opportunity to choose. They want to leave the country either by hook or by crook because they believe nothing is working out in the country any longer. They are very tired of staying the more. They want to go to a place where there are fresh greener pastures.

Some have vowed that even if it will take them one full year to get to the country of their choice that they will get there. They sleep dreaming of the country they have in mind to be. All these are because of hardship and youth unemployment in the country. So many Nigerian youths have gone abroad and they are doing well over there.

Even though some of them are not doing quality jobs in abroad, they prefer to do any one offered to them, so far there is employment in the country they migrated to. Some Nigerian youths that reside in Europe work there as morticians but they do the works over there happily because they get their pays the way it suppose to be.

Young Nigerians that are abroad are breaking grounds. Irrespective of the fact that the countries they moved to are not their country of origin, they do their best to make things work out properly. They are filled with passion and they show that through the works they do.

There are many good stories of Nigerian youths who are doing greater things in developed countries of the world who suffer less of unemployment. This is evident in the news that broke out in September 2018. Silas Adekunle, a 26-year-old Nigerian, credited for building the world's first gaming robot, has just become the highest paid in the field of Robotic engineering. Adekunle achieved this feat after signing a new deal with the world's reputable software manufacturers, Apple Inc. The robotics engineer was also named as "Someone to Watch in 2018" by the Black Hedge Fund Group, according to reports by *thebossnewspapers.com.*

Adekunle is currently the founder and CEO of Reach Robotics, a company developing the world's first gaming robots. He also recently graduated with a 1st class degree and has four years' background in robotics (Leadership 2018).

Youth unemployment in the country has pushed our great talents to the other parts of the world. They move from their fatherland to another man's land because the country they originally belong do not value them.

It is difficult to visit any country on the planet earth without seeing at least a Nigerian. They travel a lot. All these movements are because they search for greener pastures. Nigerians settle in any land where they find the green lives they look for. So many Nigerians migrate from the country to another because they want to survive. The leaders of the country instead of putting the country in order are making it hard for the citizens. It is a big issue that Nigerians do not know whom to complain to.

Some of the best health workers in the United States of America are from Nigeria. They carry out their works diligently without much stress. They do their jobs and get their pays as of when due unlike the quarrel and series of long strike observed in Nigeria before health workers are paid. These are the people that take care of human lives. They deserve to be given special treatment but the country does not consider that in most cases.

A report was published on Vanguard Newspaper on the migration of medical doctors from the country. The report from the news reporting company stated that 227 doctors migrated from Nigeria in 12 months. Globally, free movement of highly skilled professionals and experts is a positive thing. However, the cost to the home nations of migrating professionals is incalculable in terms of development opportunities and loss of investment (Akintayo Eribake 2015). Writing on the topic, Akintayo further stated "UNESCO defines brain drain as an abnormal form of scientific exchange between countries, characterized by a one-way flow in favour of the most highly developed countries. Brain drain occurs in two ways. The first is the outright and direct out migration. The second refers to when graduates trained abroad refuse to return home.

Why are these great men and woman trained to help impact the country positively leaving? Does it mean that there are so many doctors in the country to the extent that their services may not be needed? These and many others are some of the questions that someone may be battling with.

Though their leaving from the country is a loss of investment to the country but some of them believe that there will be no underpayment of their services when they find themselves in the developed countries. They do not want to pass through the stress of carrying certificates from one hospital to the other in the name of search for jobs. It is rare to see medical doctors unemployed in developed parts of the world but it can happen in Nigeria.

Anything is possible in this country. A visit to government hospitals in the country will show you that the services of medical doctors are lacking but yet our government find it difficult to employ enough hands into the system. We throw away precious things we have in this country and they are making waves in the other countries where they find themselves as their services are well appreciated over there.

The country Nigeria is passing through brain drain. Men who are to help grow the country to certain level because of how knowledgeable they are migrate to other countries due to the mismanagement in the country. When the citizens have serious health challenge and travel to abroad for treatment, some of our professionals are the one that treat them but in another man's land. Is that not a shame?

Poor management and so many other factors including the fear of being unemployed have made our students move to United States for continuous study. A report released on November 17,2015 by the Institute of International Education (IIE) disclosed that a total of 9,494 Nigerian students are currently studying in colleges and universities in the United States. The overall number of international students in American colleges and universities increased by 10 per cent to a record high of 974,926 in the 2014/2015 academic year, the highest rate in 35 years, according to the IIE's Open Doors Report on International Educational Exchange.

According to the report from UNESCO in 2016, 3,300 Nigerian students study in Ukraine and 777students study in Russia in the same year. Hungary as a country attracted over 1,000 Nigerian students. The University of Debrecen alone has about 700 Nigerian students studying in it as reported by UNESCO in 2016. About 1,755 Nigerian students were reported studying in United Arab Emirates (UAE) in 2016. Even Ghana a neighbouring country has attracted and welcomed many Nigerian students to study in their country. From the same source and same year, there were 13,919 Nigerian students that studied in Ghana.

In Canada, 3, 257 Nigerian students study in the country while 17,

973 studied in United Kingdom. Malaysia is becoming an education hub for many citizens of Nigeria. The country (Nigeria) is losing talents and money to other countries because of poor leadership and organization. According to the report from Vanguard Newspaper of Nigeria, there are about 13,000 Nigerian students studying in Malaysia.

Unpatriotic and Disloyalty

Not only that our citizens migrate to other countries where they invest their knowledge and labour to make the area they occupy better but are also disloyal to their country of origin. Disloyalty as used here is the opposite of patriotism. So many Nigerians abroad are ashamed to say that they are from Nigeria. They believe that the country is not doing well and that is why they moved to the country they occupy presently. That is one of the effects of youth unemployment. Many young men and women abroad are not proud of Nigeria.

From the voice of Mannir Dan-Ali, "I suppose patriotism is not the sort of thing that excites a lot of us. In fact any talk of patriotism is likely to induce a yawn or suspicion about the motive of the person raising it (Mannir Dan-Ali 2010)". Nigerians both home and abroad are not happy of the country. They are angry and not proud of the country. The unpatriotic attitude still boils down to the issue of youth unemployment in the country. Unpatriotic behaviour of Nigerians is an effect of youth unemployment in the country.

Ask an average Nigerian on his view on whether he can protect the country sincerely and he will ask you what the country has done for him to do that. He will tell you that nothing is working out in the country and therefore cannot be stupid to protect the country with sincerity. Some prefer to even pray for another country than Nigeria.

Witnesses have shown that some Nigerians recite the slogan "God bless America" but find it difficult to say same concerning Nigeria. The bitterness that many Nigerians have towards the country is much. Some of the citizens abroad are ashamed to identify with other citizens over there. There is disunity and disloyalty. Many Nigerian youths see praying for Nigeria as a country as throwing holy thing to a dog. To them, Nigeria has nothing good to talk about.

Increase in the number of dependent people

If you are a worker in Nigeria, you will find out that you are not using the salary paid to you on monthly basis all alone. You carry the burden of others because of the challenge of unemployment in the country. Sometimes when some phone numbers called you, your heart skips because the aim for the caller may be to demand some money from you. The calls most times come from friends or relations who are unemployed.

They are jobless citizens of the country. They call for financial support. The pay may not be much but there are so many opened hands seeking for help from the same small salary. That is where the adverse effect of youth unemployment comes in.

There is joy when parents see their children they trained in school do work and earn good money after their graduation. In this state, the children do not only make money for their spending but also give to their parents as ways to show their gratitude. But it is heart breaking when the children their parents trained in school turned and start asking for money from their parents after their graduation.

Every man wants to be independent. Both the youths and the adults want to be on their own and it is good. They want to have their own apartment, have their own cars, build their own house and acquire their own properties. But when there is high unemployment challenge, these desires may not be achieved so easily. The difficulty is due to the adverse effect of the challenge under discussion.

Even when they earn well, the demand from relations and friends can make it difficult for them to set the standard they planned. If the working youth has a plan to buy landed property for about $1,500 by next month when paid, the money may not be complete again when pressing demands come from others. His plan may be to add money from his yet to be paid salary to the money he saved before. There are some delicate demands that one cannot say no to and when they come in at the time you want to kick start a particular project, that your project can be paused. Many Nigerians are dependent of those who are working because they do not have good jobs to earn from. The effect of youth unemployment is felt through this means.

2.5 Solutions to youth unemployment

Ideas rule the world. So many world challenges that so many countries were facing years ago that have been addressed to some extent came from sound ideas. Here, we will be discussing some sound ideas that will go a long way to resolve the challenge of youth unemployment in Nigeria. The solutions to youth unemployment in the Federal Republic of Nigeria are:

- Restructuring of Nigerian Education

- Early skill acquisition

- Youth empowerment

- Consistency in power supply

- Attracting foreign investors

- Exploitation of natural and mineral resources

- Mentorship

- Youth involvement in politics

- Cutting down the salaries and allowances of Nigerian politicians

- Agriculture and proper orientation

Restructuring of Nigerian Education

It is important to change the way students are taught in the universities and other institutions of higher learning. So many things need to be changed. Let it not be all theories as usual.

Integrating sound practical into their study will go a long way in helping them understand the applications of their causes of study in real life. When they understand this fully, they can establish themselves even after graduation.

A student that studies mechanical engineering for example should not just be loaded with theories in that course. He should not just stay in the lecture hall learning how to balance forces and the rest mathematically. That will not help the youth unemployment challenge in any way. He needs things that are more than that. Things that are applicable in real life are more important.

Also, the university board should not make it that the only time to learn practical application of the course is during industrial training. That is very wrong. It is wrong in the sense that the six months industrial training given to students is not enough. Even upon that, some of the students for the training do not take part in it.

During the industrial training, some of the students just go home and relax with their loved ones. They watch videos and catch fun for the whole of six months. Due to poor monitoring by the industrial training supervisors, they do not know that those whom they think are going through industrial training are not.

At the end of the claimed training by some of the students, they forge reports and submit to the school. They are score credit or even excellent irrespective of the fact that they did not go to the field for the training. Some of those students who did not even go through the training even make better grades than those that passed through the training in some companies. What a mess in the education sector of Nigeria?

Structuring the education system of Nigeria should involve practical at least once every two weeks. This will go a long way in instilling the practical background the youths need for survival after graduation. Skill acquisition is very important to every youth that want to get employed in the real world. The author explained the "Importance of Skill Acquisition" in his article on Hubpages Inc, United States.

A student that studies Metallurgical and Materials engineering for example can go for training in any nearby welders shop close to him once every two weeks. This should be followed by proper monitoring by a lecturer in the same department to make sure he learns the welding. With this skill, he will stand out and be employable after graduation. The reason at this point is that he has an employable skill. Even when some companies do not hire him, he can hire himself because he has the needed skills to make money on his own.

The teaching materials by the teachers need to be updated. If you are conversant with the recent Android phones, you will notice that sometimes you are notified to update your applications. The essence of sending the notifications to you to update the applications is because some new features have been integrated into the App. After the update, the applications work much better.

In the same way, some teachers and lecturers that teach in different institutions need to update their teaching materials. This will make the students to be updated with what work in the current world. In the field of computer for example, there was a time when HTML was known to be the major language used in computer programming and website designing. But recently, the latest of the HTML is HTML 5. This language has some beautiful features more than the former and therefore students need to be updated with that.

There are still some other changes that have taken place in other areas of learning over the years. These updates have been in use in Europe, America and other developed parts of the world. But here in Nigeria, our lecturers have not effect these changes. We need to make these changes so that our youths can function effectively in the real world and help reduce unemployment in the country. New and classy approaches are needed in our education system.

Early skill acquisition

When you do something over and over again, you become used to such thing. In fact, that becomes part and parcel of you. That is how people become experts in a particular field. So, to start early is a key to overall human development.

In the area of coding, at the early stage of learning, it appears cumbersome as if it is not what somebody can do. When learning HTML coding for example, it seems as if it is not what someone can do off hand but when mastery is achieved, you can write those codes without looking at someone. To start early with strong dedication gives mastery as the result.

Early skill acquisition by Nigerian youths is another approach to tackle the issue of unemployment among the young ones in the society. If a young man or woman has passion in electronics, he can get linked up with people that specialize in the sector. If he is interested in the repair of electronics products, the parents or the guardians should make it a point of duty to take him to technicians that do that as their works. This attitude will make the young understand the job well. When he fully develops himself in the area, he can open a workshop of his own. He will have much customers because he started on time and will not experience unemployment challenge.

In the same view, if a young lady likes buying and selling, she can nurture such skill. The parents have a great role to play in this scenario. They should help by establishment of good relationship with people that trade in a particular commodity. This calls for early youth development. If our country is filled with young people that are well experienced in one skill or the other, the high rate of unemployment among the youths will be a history.

Every youth must not pass through university or institutions of higher learning. It is basic for skills to be part of every youth in a particular society. There is high unemployment in the country among Nigerian youths because everybody wants to attend higher institutions. Parents should not force their children to go to the universities. If any wants to learn how to do business, allow him or her so long he or she is of the age to make decision of their own. What is more important is that at the end, they secure jobs and they live well. There are many unemployed youths because some did not know their left from their right when they were in school.

Go to the cities in the country and see great things people are doing. You can visit Onitsha in Anambra state, Lagos state, Abuja city, Kaduna, and Kano and see what young men and women are doing with money. Also, some adults are doing well in their individual businesses. Do you know the surprising thing? Many of them; be them adults or youths did not pass through higher educations. Some served their masters for about six years before they were sponsored to start their own businesses in their areas of expertise.

They were trained and today they do well because they acquired their business skills early. Most of them are from Igbo, one of the major tribes in Nigeria. Some of them began to learn from their masters immediately after their secondary school at their tender ages. They got the ideas right from when they were young and employ themselves and they manage their individual businesses on their own. They are not well educated but they live large. They did not pass through higher formal education but they are richer than those that attended higher educations. Do not underestimate the power of early skill acquisition.

Youth empowerment

Some of the Nigeria youths are helpless. They need assistance and support. You can impact your ideas into any of them. Youth empowerment has helped many people discover who they are and things they can do.

You can be of a great help. You can teach any youth around you how to write, how to write code, and how to repair technically. Do not say he may not be able to do it. Just teach that youth first. What you teach him today may be a great source of livelihood to him till the end of his living on the planet earth. An empowered youth stands a great chance of succeeding greatly in a society than when he is not empowered at all.

According to Definition.net, youth empowerment is an attitudinal, structural, and cultural process whereby young people gain the ability, authority, and agency to make decisions and implement change in their own lives and the lives of other people, including youth and adults. Youth empowerment is often addressed as a gateway to intergenerational equity, civic engagement and democracy building (Definition.net 2005).

One of the ways to empower the youths is giving them the opportunity to take part in politics and decision making in the country. When the leaders of the country stop buying their ways in to the leadership positions of the country and allow the youths to participate, they will help in making policies that will help the youths establish themselves more and stop suffering the rot of unemployment. If the government officers in the country should stay away from corrupt practices which includes rigging during elections and empower the youths to assume some government positions, the youths will breathe in fresh air. Allowing them into top positions is a means of empowering the youths.

Youth empowerment can affect the attitudes of the youths positively. A situation where rich men and women in country decide to sponsor the young people in their communities with some amount of money to start any business of their choice will help. An action of this kind will help make the youths in the country live well.

Also, the government and non-governmental organizations can help empower the young people in Nigeria. The empowerment can come in so many forms. They can build skill acquisition centres in parts of the country where the youths are taught some paying skills in the recent time.

When the youths are empowered skilfully and they start making it in life, they can empower others as well. With time, the country will be occupied with network of youths that are empowered and empowering others to resolve unemployment problem. Agricultural empowerment is not exempted.

Consistency in power supply

The term consistency stands for the quality of always being the same, doing things in the same way, having the same standards. The state of power supply in the country has to be of good standard and consistence. It will make things work out well and the challenge of youth unemployment in the country will be addressed.

When there is consistent power supply in the country, there will be more production. Higher production means higher demand of human labour. This demand of human labour gives room for employing of more youths in the production sections of the country.

When there is constant supply of power, the youths who manage small and medium businesses will sustain them. They will not spend the money they are to use in equipping of their businesses on gasoline and diesel. Instead, they use the money for the expansion of their businesses which give opportunity for employment of other young men and women in our society.

Some companies are not producing enough today because of the challenge posed by power supply in the country. If the government of the country can team together and solve the issue, there will be open doors of employment for the young. When the doors are opened, many Nigerian youths will embrace the opportunity offered by constant power supply in the country.

There are some businesses that youths that are interested in entrepreneurship would have loved to go into but power challenge stopped them. Example of such is selling of frozen foods. There is gain in the business. A lot of youths are willing to dive into the business if the issue of power supply is resolved. Consistency in the supply of power nationwide will help make the job easier for the youths.

In the other way, it will make them make more profit. With this profit, they can establish other branches within the city. As the branches are established, more jobs are created for the citizens of the country including the youths. Youths can ask for soft loans and start some businesses when they know they will not spend much on avenues to generate power, maybe by buying of electric generators and fuelling with gasoline. In the fight to solve the challenge of power in Nigeria, experienced engineers are needed.

Attracting foreign investors

It is time for Nigeria government to stand up and make a move. The move they should make is to bring foreign investors into the country. This will go a long way to reduce the suffering of our young men and women in the country.

There are many imported goods we make use of in this country. These goods in question can be produce in Nigeria to strengthen the economy of the country in return. For example, canned Sardines (canned food which the main contents are fish and sauce) are imported mainly from Morocco. This product sells so much in the Federal Republic of Nigeria. You cannot fully comprehend how much the companies that make this product generate from Nigeria every day. It is an edible material so people must buy it every day.

Is it too difficult for the government of Nigeria to reach an agreement with the companies that produce this food to come and build their companies here is Nigeria and continue with their

111

production? If they build their companies here in Nigeria, it will boost the economy of the country. Also, it will open door for more youths to secure jobs in the country.

Our government have to be up and doing. There are so many companies that are willing to come and invest in the country. But our leaders need to make a move for this to be achieved. They have to look around and take record of the items that may not be easily produced here and then get those companies into the country to help solve some of the issues faced by the citizens.

Exploitation of natural and mineral resources

Nigeria is blessed. We have the resources needed to make this country one of the world best. The country is rich in natural and mineral resources. If these resources are exploited adequately, the issue of youth unemployment in Nigeria will be a history. In fact the high demand for labour will make the youths make choices of what they want and what they do not want. In this state, there will be job satisfaction.

There are many imported furniture products in the country. The woods through which the furniture products are made from are not lacking in the country. Nigeria has good forests to source the woods needed for these furniture products of any kinds and styles.

Companies that produce these products can be established in the country to make these products even at lower cost. These products should be banned from being imported from outside countries. China and Malaysia where these products usually come from do not have better woods than Nigeria. Exploitation of the trees in the country for making of standard furniture products will result to building companies that make such products. These companies in return will employ the youths that will use their commitment to make the economy of the country better.

Ajaokuta Steel Company should have been a huge source of employment to the youths and many citizens of Nigeria. Nigeria has the raw materials for the production of steel. What is needed is good management of this company and employment will be available. This great company can be revived again.

Ajaokuta Steel Company Limited (ASCL) popularly known as Ajaokuta Steel Mill is a steel mill in Nigeria, located in Ajaokuta, Kogi State, Nigeria. Built on a 24,000 hectares (59,000 acres) site started in 1979, it is the largest steel mill in Nigeria, and the coke oven and by products plants are larger than all the refineries in Nigeria combined. Thought the steel mill has not commenced work properly, it will be a great source of joy to the country.

One of the ways in which it will be a source of joy is through employment generation. The company is a large one. The reason for the establishment of the company in the country is because the country is rich in iron ore. Iron ore is a major component of steel. Exploitation of this natural resource will create good opportunities for the youths in the country. Steel is an alloy of iron and carbon and other elements. Because of its high tensile strength and low cost, it is a major component used in buildings, infrastructure, tools, ships, automobiles, machines, appliances, and weapons. Iron is the base metal of steel.

There are countries that have been growing their GDP (Gross Domestic Product) from the revenue generated from sale of steel worldwide. Nigeria as a country can join the market and compete with the countries that have been in existence. According to Statista, China is the largest producer of steel in the world in the year 2017. U.S steel imports peaked in 2015, when the trade deficit reached 745.66 billion U.S. dollars (Statista 2016). Nigeria can make it big if Ajaokuta Steel Company Limited is fixed and made functioning. Youths will be employed and the economy will be revived as well.

Steel has a lot of applications in the society today. Not only that the country will make use of the steel alloys produced in the company but the products will also be exported to other countries. The produced steel will be of standard quality and can stand the test of time. If this investment is properly maintained, we will start competing with countries that have that as their major source of revenue with time.

There are so many other mineral and natural resources in Nigeria that can be exploited to get our youths employed. Cocoa for instance is a major fruit that can be used for the manufacturing of tea and coffee. The country does not need to import these items again. What is important is deep exploitation of the raw material used for the production and overtime there will be surplus of "made in Nigeria" tea and coffee.

In the mid 19th century, Nigeria's agricultural industry provided jobs to over 70% of the population. The primary product was cocoa, and the success of the market was immortalized in Cocoa House in Ibadan, Oyo state, a house named for the successful crop that funded its existence. According to MIT's Observatory of Economic Complexity (OEC), cocoa is among Nigeria's top exports. Though it only represents 2% of the nation's exports, the cocoa bean is the third largest export from Nigeria after crude petroleum and petroleum gas. Cocoa exports are a $740 Million USD industry in Nigeria (Amira Daoui 2018).

Kaolin is a good natural resource found in Nigeria. This is found in many states in Nigeria including Delta and Ekiti states. Exploitation of this material made available by nature can create more jobs for the young men and women in the country. It also has many applications and that will make the material to sell more.

It has cosmetics and health applications. It is used for the production of insecticide and papers. In terms of its cosmetics application, kaolin is used to produce cream. And in the health application, it is used to treat diarrhea. It is a good material. Companies can be built by entrepreneurs when kaolin is sourced and sold both locally and internationally.

Mentorship

The young needs at least a mentor. There are people out there that can take the youths as mentees and teach things they need to know to be free from the rot of unemployment in the society and do better in life. It is key and is helpful in human development in totality.

Standing on the shoulders of giants can help one to see farer than the height the person might be ordinarily if he stands on his or her own. Our young people need people they will lean on to source for knowledge. They need people they will lean on to have clear view of where they are going to find themselves. It is empowering and great to have a mentor.

Experience is the best teacher as people say. Someone that is more experienced than a young person can go a long way to give the young tips to break ground in a particular area. If he loves you, he takes you as his own and has nothing to hide from you. He opens his heart and allows you to come in to learn some new ideas.

It is not necessarily compulsory for the youths to go to coaching or mentorship school before he or she can have a mentor. Based on the topic and the context under discussion, that is wrong. You can have a mentor even when you do not go to any mentoring school.

Your uncle or your friend can be your mentor. You will become his mentee in this case. Your friend whom you see as a friend can be a mentor to you when you discover some unique things from him and want to learn to establish yourself.

He can teach you and at the end what you learnt from him becomes a source of livelihood to you. Be humble and flexible to coach you and do that well. Irrespective of his age, just be humble and allow him to impart great paying ideas into you.

Some mentors are like second parents, so go closer to them and they will take you as their own. No matter how hard the Nigeria economy seems to be, they are always ready to assist. They can link you up with some companies that will employ you and pay you well. They are your coach and so want the best for you.

In the world of football, there are footballers who are doing great things. These are men that are being respected so much by both football fans and those who are not football lovers. But do you know the surprising thing? These young football stars had coaches that made whom they are today. Even before they reach to the height of playing in football clubs recognized globally as standard one, somebody groomed them at the younger age.

Those who coached them at those small ages when nobody knew them gave them lift to be linked up to higher clubs. When they got to the club that was higher than the one they were before, another coach or mentor trained them. And that new mentor promoted them until they got to another bigger club that sampled them to the entire world to see. Behind any successful footballer there is always a mentor. That is a fact.

Cristiano Ronaldo a Portuguese national footballer and former Real Madrid player is where he is where he is today because he had a mentor/coach right from when he was younger than his present age. Will you say that he is unemployed? That is impossible because he himself is an employer of labour including the youths.

Cristiano Ronaldo is one of the richest athletes in the world. The

33-year-old Real Madrid soccer star has an estimated net worth of $450 million. As of June 5, 2018, the Portugal-born soccer star has already made an estimated $108 million for the year, according to Forbes. About $61 million came from his salary, bonuses and winnings, and his endorsement deals brought in an additional $47 million (Darren Geeter 2018).

On 12 September 2018, it was announced that the hotel group of the footballer will be opening a new hotel in Paris, France. The Portuguese hotel group, Pestana, announced on Wednesday that they will open a new hotel in Paris with Cristiano Ronaldo's name, Pestana CR7 Hotel, in which they have invested €60 million. The hotel is set to potentially open in 2021 (Agunbiade Sanya 2018). Mentorship is one of the major contributors of the success of the young footballer today. It can also be a source of open door to create employment for Nigerian youths. It can be a way to reduce youth unemployment in Nigeria.

Youth involvement in politics

Nigeria is a country where the elderly in the society wants to stay in power till their death. Even when they are dying, they want to die holding the power. Even in the land of the death, they still want to rule there. Once upon a time, a president of Nigeria after travelling to London and other parts of the world due to his critical health challenge was advised to leave power for the younger vice to takeover, he kicked against the advice to continue with his leadership. He felt he could continue with the leadership and felt like a young man not knowing he was due for such political position.

As of the time of writing of this section of this book (December 2018), this president of the Federal Republic of Nigeria is 75 years. That is the official age of the man. What can a man of 75 years do? Can he absorb the stress coming to the presidency? He is tired and need to be somewhere relaxing and being taken care by the children and grandchildren. The most annoying thing is that this president at this age of 75 years still wants to contest for second tenure in the same national presidency post.

What percentage of Nigerian youths are holding leadership position in Nigerian Federal leadership positions? What percentage of youths are occupying political positions in the government of the country as a whole? They are just very few.

Because the number of these young men and women in politics are very few, their needs do not count in some cases. When the old men in the top leadership positions of the country are making new policies, they sometimes overlook the needs of the young men and women in the country. This is why they make policy that at the end do not favour the youths. This is because the youths are not occupying some decision making positions in the federal government.

When you are in a particular age bracket, you know and understand how the people in that group act. Also, you know the pain they feel. This will make you do anything within your power to attend to the needs of these young people because you are part of the people whom are in that bracket.

It will be nice for the members of House of Senate to revisit the constitution of the country. After which some senatorial positions should be declared open for the youths of the country to occupy. This will make the youths to have a say in decision making in the country.

The young in the country should be carried along in political dialogue. The youths occupy high number in terms of population in the country. If not for any reason, they should be given some positions in federal government. They have to strongly take part.

The participation of youths in political positions will make them enforce policies that will go a long way to solve youth challenges. One of the challenges which are under discussion is the youth unemployment. Their participation will create and enforce ideas that will arrest youth unemployment in the country. We are part of this country so we need to fully participate in decision making of any kind in the country.

Reducing the salaries and allowances of Nigerian politicians

How can a Nigerian senator earn over two million United States Dollars in a year? Is that not wickedness in the highest order. It is cruel. They are pretending to be leaders while they are blood suckers. The senators of the Federal Republic of Nigeria are parasites. They are eating down the economy of the country and increasing unemployment among the youths of the country.

One of the major ways to reduce youth unemployment is by cutting down the money paid to Nigerian politicians as salaries and allowances on monthly and yearly basis. When this is done, the money will be used for infrastructural development in the country. In return, these established places will employ the youths.

What is the comparison between the Gross Domestic Product of Nigeria with that of United States of America? The margin is very high. It is time for the senators in Nigeria to tell themselves the truth. America is much richer than Nigeria and yet Nigerian senators pay themselves more than those of United States of America. There is need for immediate reduction of the payment made to these men and women in politics.

The money cut out from their initial pay can be invested into other areas. They can be used to build manufacturing companies that will take young people with great ideas. Also, football pitches can be built in the country. The standard of such pitches can result to employing Nigerians that will work there.

Also, the youths can earn their living from there and be employed. There are only few standard hospitals in the country. Establishing at least three standard hospitals that each can accommodate at least five thousand patients will open door to many youths in the country. These hospitals cannot only employ young health workers but also people that specialize in other disciplines.

A hospital of that standard will have engineers, cleaners, security officers, plumbers, and the rest. An electrical engineer in the hospital of this kind will check and maintain electrical related areas in the hospital. Mechanical engineers also have their roles to play in the hospital. They are to make sure that all the mechanical machines in the hospital are in good state. The engineers are hired as permanent staff because some duties may require their immediate attentions.

On the other hand, there must be enough cleaners in the hospitals. Hygiene is of paramount importance in hospitals, therefore the departments and patient wards in the hospitals must be kept clean always. To this effect, enough cleaners are to be employed and this also reduces the rate of unemployment among youths in the country.

Plumbers find their usefulness in hospitals be it big or small ones. Because of this, the established hospitals which will come into existence as a result of reduction of the monthly and yearly pay of Nigerian politicians will employ many Nigerian young plumbers. They will do their jobs including maintenance and get their pay at the right time.

Agriculture and proper orientation

Everyone needs food for survival. You as a reader of this book need food to survive. Without proper feeding, you will dry up one day. That is what makes agriculture precious. No matter how bad an economy may seems to be, people must still buy food and eat which is an agricultural produce.

Youths' involvement in agriculture is a solution to youth unemployment. It is a simple way of making money to feed the masses. Before the discovery of crude oil which happens to be the major source of income to the nation today, the country had agriculture as her major source of income. They invest in agriculture heavily and had good return in terms of profit then.

In the 1960s, before it turned to oil, Nigeria was one of the most promising agricultural producers in the world. Between 1962 and 1968, export crops were the country's main foreign exchange earner. The country was number one globally in palm oil exports, well ahead of Malaysia and Indonesia, and exported 47 percent of all groundnuts, putting it ahead of the US and Argentina.

But the country's status as agricultural products powerhouse has declined and steeply. While Nigeria once provided 18 percent of the global production of cocoa, second in the world in the 1960s, that figure is now down to 8 percent. And while the country produces 65 percent of tomatoes in West Africa, it is now the largest importer of tomato paste (Adam Robert Green 2013). It is a pity but the youths can make it happen again.

They can take agriculture as their jobs and make good sum of money from the practice. There are a lot of advantages in being a farmer. One is that you do not lack food. You feed large population of people and they are happy about that. You have your freedom and enough time to rest unlike when you are employed in a corporate organization where you stay all day till evening before you are allowed to go home by your manager. In agriculture practice, you can make more money than when you are just a salary earner that gets paid once in a month.

Our youths' involvement in agriculture will really employ them and at the same time be a source of revival to the country's economy. The country will gain much through this idea. The youths are energetic and they can make things happen. They have the potentials to do that.

The government of Nigeria have to come in to make this work to its optimal level. They have to reach agreement with people that have large hectares of land which are not in use. The agreement will be to leave their land for the promotion of agricultural practice by the youths of the country. Also they have to pay some money to communities that have these lands to avoid dispute. The payment can be made yearly to the community that has the land. The payments are made as compensation to the communities. They later share the money among the individuals that have the lands that are used by the youths for agriculture.

When a youth for example acquire some lands for agriculture and plant 5,000 plantain trees on it, you will be surprised on the gain the youth will make during harvest. He may not sell those produce locally but internationally as well. Within some time, he becomes exporter of agricultural produce. What a boast and employment. There are still other crops they can go into including planting of palm trees to source palm oil.

Another important thing is orientation. Orientation creates awareness for people who do not know much about a particular thing or idea. During orientation, people get to know what they do not know before and grow in knowledge. It is a powerful tool for human growth and development.

The way a youth may perceive agriculture may not really be it until he passes through training on that area. This will make him or her learn the new tools and skills needed to make huge return in being a farmer. Orientation is designed to provide a new employee with the information he or she needs to function comfortably and effectively in a particular area. When youths pass through proper training on agriculture, they will take it as their jobs and do well. It will be helpful and the youths that will be going into agriculture suggested as one of the ways to reduce youth unemployment need to pass through a proper orientation proven to be one of the weapons many businesses have used to succeed in many communities.

2.6 Youth Empowering Organizations in Nigeria

According to Kelvin Okafor of Legit, youth empowerment is a process where children and young people are encouraged to take charge of their lives. They do this by addressing their situation and then take action in order to improve their access to resources and transform their consciousness through their beliefs, values and attitudes (Kelvin Okafor 2017).

Irrespective of high unemployment in Nigeria, there are organizations that exist in and outside the country to empower the youths of the country. Some of these youth empowering group do not only support and encourage the youths but also other citizens of the country that have passed youthful age. In this section, we will be discussing some groups that have empowered the youths in Nigeria. Some of these organizations are discovered and powered by philanthropists.

Youth Empowerment Programme (YEP)

The project was co-funded by United Nations Development Program (UNDP), Shell Petroleum Development Company (SPDC) and Delta state government. This group of youth empowerment is created to address the challenge of youth unemployment and poverty in the country especially in Niger Delta areas. The Niger Delta areas are the oil producing states in the Federal Republic of Nigeria.

Due to oil spillage in these states that produce crude oil in Nigeria, some of the lands are not productive any longer in terms of agriculture. They are not productive in the sense that they are not good for growing of crops again. Plants cannot grow on the lands again. Because of this, some Nigerian youths that specialize in agricultural practice could not plant their crops any longer. This leaves many number of them unemployed. In order to address this and other crises that have been going on in these Niger Delta areas, empowerment programmes were set up. Youth Empowerment Programmes are introduced to help reduce the challenge among the youths. Niger Delta areas (oil producing states) in Nigeria are Akwa Ibom, Delta, Rivers, Bayelsa, Ondo, Edo, Imo and Abia.

YEP is a mindset changing programme that has changed a good number of youths in the Niger-Delta region. This project has helped in controlling the crises in Niger Delta by engaging idle youths in meaningful jobs. This programme has created an avenue for poverty reduction in Niger-Delta region - Legit.

The programme Youth Empowerment Programme (YEP) had a very positive impact on the lives of many of the youth in the community (Apostle Opuama 2013). This program has empowered the youths both skilfully and financially. Through it many youths have been sent to institutes where they learnt important skills and through that employ themselves by setting up businesses on areas they are trained.

Some after learning skills like welding are also given financial support by the group to start workshops of their own. It has really helped many youths in Nigeria. The skills that the empowerment programme impact into are but not limited to welding and fabrication, electrical and electronics repair, teaching skills, safety, catering, acting, plumbing and pipefitting.

N-Power

N-Power is a youth empowerment programme in Nigeria that has her slogan as "Empowering Nigerian Youths for Prosperity". The group was created to empower the youths of the Federal Republic of Nigeria from the major challenge they face in the country. And that major challenge is nothing else but youth unemployment.

In the about section of the youth empowerment organizations, it stated "Skills and knowledge are the driving forces of economic growth and social development. Despite the current high level of unemployment, harnessing Nigeria's young demography through

135

appropriate skill development efforts provides an opportunity to achieve inclusion and productivity within the country. Large-scale skill development is the main policy thrust of the N-Power Programme.

N-Power is also linked to the Federal Government's policies in the economic, employment and social development arenas. N-Power addresses the challenge of youth unemployment by providing a structure for large scale and relevant work skills acquisition and development while linking its core and outcomes to fixing inadequate public services and stimulating the larger economy. The modular programmes under N-Power will ensure that each participant will learn and practice most of what is necessary to find or create work".

Within two years of operation of this organization, it has trained over 500,000 (five hundred thousand) Nigeria youths. They concentrate in empowering Nigerian youths within 18 to 35 years.Government of Nigeria pay beneficiaries of this program as they learn skills which is believed to revive the country in one way or the other. The essence of the payment is to enable them gather money as they learn adequate skills. With the money saved within the period of their learning, they are expected to use them start business of their own and stop being unemployed.

There are many skills learnt under this program by the youths. The skills include teaching, software development, computer hardware, agriculture, health, tax compliance, animation, graphics design, script writing, building services, constructions and automotive. The unemployed youths are linked with companies that special in these services to learn the skills.

In application into N-Power youth empowerment programme, any youth who is already employed in a particular establishment cannot be taken by the group. This is because Nigerian youths that are unemployed are the people needed by the scheme organizer. Youths who are already having jobs that pay them are advised to stick to their jobs so that they do not occupy the space of others that are unemployed.

During the application into the program, Bank Verification Numbers (BVN) of the applicants are needed. This is to verify the applicants and also to check the accounts to know if they receive regular income. That is to say that the BVN is used to verify the youths details and for adequate confirmation. Also, BVN is used to confirm the real name of the applicants. The name on the credentials of the benefactors must match the names on their BVN before they are paid during the training. The youths that make it after application will have their names published on newspapers and also on the N-Power website.

Tony Elumelu Foundation

Tony Elumelu is a man of vision and of the people. He is a great philanthropist whose positive impact is not only felt in Nigeria but in the other African countries. He is a man respected by the entire African countries. Elumelu through his foundation has empowered a lot of African youths that have unique ideas to present to the world to make it a better place for all.

He is from Onicha-Ukwu in Aniocha North Local Government Area of Delta state and his impact is felt in his own state. According to Wikipedia, Tony OnyemaechiElumelu (born 22 March 1963) is a Nigerian economist, entrepreneur, and philanthropist. He is the chairman of Heirs Holdings, the United Bank for Africa, Transcorp and founder of The Tony Elumelu Foundation. Elumelu holds the Nigerian national honours, the Commander of the Order of the Niger (CON) and Member of the Order of the Federal Republic (MFR). He was recognised as one of "Africa's 20 Most Powerful People in 2012" by Forbes magazine.

As of December 2018, Tony Elumelu foundation is the leading philanthropy in Africa championing entrepreneurship. Once the applicant has exceptional entrepreneurship ideas and applies with clean presentation of his or her ideas, he or she is likely to be taken after the final judgment by Tony Elumelu Foundation team. In

2018 alone, the foundation received total of 151,692 applications from contestants from different countries in African Continent.

The foundation was established in the year 2010. The governments of various countries have commended the work the foundation is doing to make the lives of many Africans better by given those who are business minded financial support to make them expand Africa economically. The Foundation's long-term investment in empowering African entrepreneurs is emblematic of Tony Elumelu's philosophy of Africapitalism, which positions Africa's private sector and most importantly entrepreneurs, as the catalyst for the social and economic development of the continent.

The foundation believes that the economic success of Africa is locked in Small and Medium Enterprises. To the philanthropist, if these entrepreneurs are empowered with the necessary tools, Africa will stand up tall. Those empowered also include youths who manage businesses as well as those that have ideas but no fund to startup.

Because of the mindset of empowering people who will take Africa's economy to a higher level, that is the reason for the company's vision. The vision for the foundation is to unlock the obstacles that Africa's entrepreneurs face as they grow their start-ups into small to medium enterprises (SMEs), their SMEs into national growth companies, and their national growth companies into African multinationals.

The foundation has mentors. They serve as coaches to the upcoming entrepreneurs. They have helped many benefactors of the organization reach certain good marks.

Youth Enterprise with Innovation in Nigeria (YouWiN!)

YouWin! Is an organization established by the Federal Government of Nigeria in November, 2011, to help in fighting unemployment among Nigerian graduates. It sole involves an innovative business plan competition aimed at job creation by encouraging and supporting aspiring entrepreneurial youth in Nigeria to develop and execute business ideas.

The accomplishments of the 1,200 YouWiN! Awardees' were celebrated at the Presidential Villa on April 12, 2012. The organization was established during the leadership of President Goodluck Jonathan.

The competition is usually organized on November of every year and those that emerge winners are given good sum of money to start the business they wrote about during the competition. The government of the country usually organize training for the winners on the areas they want to invest in.

The reason why the government is doing so is because it understands that investing in the youths by equipping them financially and skilfully will help in generating more jobs for the rest of the citizens. Since the establishment of the project, those who were empowered have employed many Nigerians into their establishments all over the country.

The schemes that Youth Enterprise with Innovation in Nigeria (YouWIN) carry-out are diverse. It is diverse because many youths that win in the competition held by the organization have their individual areas of concentration. The schemes that the organization encourages through her winner are not limited to the following:

- Cyber Café management;

- Graphics design;

- Website design and development;

- Industrials manufacturing;

- Polymer recycling;

- Agricultural and poultry empowerment; and

- Media company establishment.

Subsidy Reinvestment and Empowerment Programme (SURE-P)

Subsidy Reinvestment and Empowerment Programme (SURE-P), is the initiation of the Government of Federal Republic of Nigeria to help both the youths and other citizens of the country. The scheme has added new breath of life into many Nigerian youths of today. Not far from what other youth empowerment organizations do, they equip the youths on lucrative skills that they need to survive in the society they live.

The fund that is used by the scheme is that generated from the resources accrued to the Federal Government as savings from the partial removal of fuel subsidy, and it is headed by Dr. Christopher Kolade. Dr. Christopher Kolade is working hard with his team members to ensure that the fund is used in development of the country for good. This organization is what gave birth to Graduate Internship Scheme which is yet to be discussed.

Youth Initiative for Sustainable Agriculture in Nigeria (YISA)

Youth Initiative for Sustainable Agriculture is centred on supporting Nigerian youths who are interested in the field of agriculture or encouraging agricultural practices among them. This organization has contributed greatly to the welfare of many Nigerian youths.

The reason for crafting out of this programme by the government

144

of Federal Republic of Nigeria is that there is burning zeal in the youths unlike what is found in the old. It is believed that the youths have all it takes to revive the agriculture sector of the country.

Before the discovery of crude oil in Nigeria, Agriculture was the major source of income in the country. Nigerians were cultivating foods in the large quantity (commercial agriculture) and export to other parts of the world.

In fact, many countries were depending on the agricultural produce of this country for their own livelihood. But today, the reverse is the case as Crude oil fund is what Nigerians and their government are interest in. In the recent time (2014), there is a report that the crude oil of the Federal Republic of Nigeria is gradually drying and the government of the country is making efforts to look into other sectors that can generate revenue to the country which is principally agriculture.

There are many varieties of agricultural products which Nigeria was exporting abroad to other countries when agricultural products was still the major source of income of the country known as the giant of Africa. Among the produce were cocoa, cotton, palm nuts/kernel, and cassava. Today, Nigeria as a nation hardly export these produce as the attention of all and sundry is geared toward oil money.

We hear of Malaysia that are making their mark in Palm kernel and palm nuts. The country got the palm nut they have all over their country today from Nigeria. They have wax so strong in using that in developing their economy and other sectors while Nigeria that gave them the seed are declining in what they empowered them in.

Facts and figure has shown that Agriculture once contributed to the economic growth of Nigeria in the early time of the country's independence (Nigeria got her independence on October 1, 960). The contribution of agriculture to the Gross Domestic Products (GDP) of Nigeria in 1960 was 63 percent of the country's economy in that year and this declined to 32 percent in 1988. In the 1960s, the agricultural sector was the most important in terms of contribution to domestic production, employment and foreign exchange earnings (National Bureau of Statistics 2014).

In 1993 at 1984 Constant Factor Cost, crops (the major source of food) accounted for about 30% of the Gross Domestic Products (GDP), livestock about 5%, forestry and wildlife about 1.3% and fisheries accounted 1.2%.

Graduate Internship Scheme (GIS)

GIS is another scheme invented by the government of the Federal Republic of Nigeria to assist and equip Nigerian youth graduates on the important skills they need to survive in the world. Nigerian graduates have suffered so many challenges posed by high unemployment in the country.

Large numbers of graduates leave the tertiary institutions in the country with the hope of securing good jobs, but they became surprised when they discovered that after three years or more of their graduations, there came no jobs for them.

Some of them made their plans that they will show their appreciations to their parents for training them for a period of four to five years when they were in universities but end up becoming ashamed as they found out they were still under their care after staying for years in the universities. To reduce this challenge, the government of Nigeria introduced this scheme for training of jobless Nigerian graduates.

The Graduate Internship Scheme **(GIS)** was launched in October, 2012 to create opportunity for graduates to be attached to firms /organizations, where they can work for a year and enjoy a monthly stipend of **N30, 000 (thirty thousand Nigeria naira)** with a **Group Life and Accident Insurance.** Such interns can use the opportunity to gain working experience and enhance their employability skills (SURE-P 2012). It is an arm of SURE-P.

The schemes covered through this include the following:

- Gaining experience on automobile repair;

- Fashion and design;

- Information Communication Technology related skills;

- Electronics repair;

- Building and architectural design;

- Manufacturing and production skills;

- Cosmetics and others.

References

- Adam R. G (2013), Agriculture is the Future of Nigeria, published by Forbes Media LLC, 499 Washington Blvd Jersey City, NJ 07310, United States

- Adekunle (2017), Nigeria only oil producing country struggling with importation of refined products – Kachikwu, published by Vanguard News, Nigeria

- After School Africa (2018), Top 10 Countries for Nigerian Students to Study Abroad and what You need to Know, published by After School Africa, Nigeria

- Agunbiade .S. (2018), Cristiano Ronaldo to open CR7 hotel in Paris, published by Lailas News, Nigeria

- Akintayo .E. (2015), 227 doctors migrated from Nigeria in 12 months — Report, published by Vanguard News, Nigeria

- Alex .N. (2013), Nepotism blamed for youth unemployment, published by East Africa, Nation Centre,

Kimathi Street, P.O. Box 49010, GPO 00100, Nairobi, Kenya

- Amira .D. (2018), How to export Cocoa from Nigeria?, published by Ways to Cap, Nigeria

- Apostle Opuama (2013), Views and Impact of Youth Empowerment Programme (YEP), published by Youth Empowerment Programme, Nigeria

- Austin .O. (2014), Youth Unemployment gave rise to Terrorism, Kidnapping in Nigeria, says Uduaghan, published by Vanguard news, Nigeria

- Ayo O. B (2018), Youth unemployment as a ticking time bomb, published by Punch Nigeria News, Nigeria

- BBC (2016), Nigerian economy slips into recession, published by British Broadcasting Corporation, United Kingdom

- Darren .G. (2018), The business of being Cristiano Ronaldo, published by Consumer News and Business

Channel (CNBC), Englewood Cliffs, New Jersey, United States

- Definition.net (2005), Definition for Youth Empowerment, published by Definition.net

- Deolu (2012), Graduate turned Armed Robber makes Shocking Confession, published by Information Nigeria, Nigeria

- Emmanuel J. N (2016), Impact of Unemployment on Nigeria economic Growth 1981-2015, published by Educacinfo, No 5 Ogui Road, Enugu state, Nigeria

- Ezie, O. (2012), Youth unemployment and its socio-economic implications in Nigeria, Journal of Social Science and Public Policy. 4: 112-119. ISSN 2277-0038, Nigeria

- Farida .W. (2010), Corruption Prevention in Public Procurement in Nigeria, published by Bureau of Public Procurement (BPP), Public Procurement Journal, Nigeria

- Federal Ministry of Youth and Sports Development (2018), Nigeria Natural Resources, Abuja, Nigeria

- John C. (2018), Uproar Over Parliamentary Salaries in Nigeria, Again, published by Council on Foreign Relations, 58 East 68th Street New York, NY 10065, United States

- Johnson .O. (2017), Understanding the challenges of unemployment in Nigeria, published by Legit, Nigeria

- Kelvin Okafor (2018), Top 10 youth empowerment programmes you can try for FREE, published by Legit, Nigeria

- Leadership (2018), 26-year Old Nigerian, Adekunle becomes World Highest Paid Robotics Engineer, published by The Leadership Agency Report, 27 Ibrahim Tahir Lane, Utako, Abuja FCT, Nigeria

- Maduawuchi (2017), Unemployment in Nigeria: Causes and Solutions, published by Nigerian Infopedia, Nigeria

- Mannir Dan-Ali (2010), Viewpoint: What it means to be Nigerian, published by BBC, United Kingdom

- Mary B. I (2016), Unemployment and Underemployment as Indices of Nigerian Youths Mental Health and the

Place of Agricultural Revolution as a Panacea: Implications for Counselling, Department of Guidance and Counselling, Faculty of Education Adekunle Ajasin University, Akungba Akoko, Ondo State, Nigeria

- Morris, S.D. (1991), Corruption and Politics in Contemporary Mexico, University of Alabama Press, Tuscaloosa

- National Bureau of Statistics Nigeria (2017), Nigeria Youth Unemployment rate, published by National Bureau of Statistics, Nigeria

- Nigerian Finder (2015), 5 Major causes of unemployment in Nigeria, published by Nigerian Finder, Nigeria

- Olanrewaju M. H (2014), Entrepreneurial Development; Panacea To Unemployment In Nigeria, Lap Lambert Academic Publishing, England

- Olawale S (2018), 10 Major Causes of unemployment in Nigeria and Solutions, published by Naija Quest, Nigeria

- Statista (2016), Steel Industry – Statistics and Facts, published by Statista, United States

- Teaching Tolerance (2012), Poverty and Unemployment: Exploring the Connections, published by Teaching Tolerance, South Poverty Law Center, 400 Washington Avenue, Montgomery, AL 36104, United States

- The Tony Elumelu Foundation (2018), The Tony Elumelu Foundation - Africa's leading PhilanthropicInstitution, published by TEF, Nigeria

- Tony (2016), Youth unemployment in Nigeria: A weapon of destruction, published by Vanguard News, Nigeria

- Transparency International (2000), Corruption Perception Index 2000, Published by Transparency International, Berlin Germany

- Uzochukwu Mike (2014), Corruption in Nigeria: Overview, Causes, Effects and Solutions, published by HubPages Inc., 1111 Broadway Floor 3, Oakland CA 94607, United States

- Ibid (2017), Causes of Poverty in Nigeria – New Approach, published by HubPages Inc., 1111 Broadway Floor 3, Oakland CA 94607, United States

Chapter 3

Drug abuse among Nigerian Youths

Drugs are good; Drugs are helpful; Drugs make us feel good when we are not sound health wise; Drugs are essential in terms of relief of our pains. Do not believe anybody that tells you that drugs are not good and important for healthy being of the human generation.

But, do you know when it is a problem? It is a problem when these drugs are abused. The abuse of drugs has been killing many Nigerian youths unknown to them. It kills quietly until it reduces the person that abuses it to nothing. There is high abuse of drugs sold in the country. The above are done by both the youths and adults that live in our community. This in one way or the other has negative effects not only on the abusers but the community at large.

"Both the range of drugs and drug markets are expanding and diversifying as never before. The findings of this year's World Drug Report make clear that the international community needs to step up its responses to cope with these challenges. We are facing a potential supply-driven expansion of drug markets, with production of opium and manufacture of cocaine at the highest levels ever recorded. Markets for cocaine and methamphetamine are extending beyond their usual regions and, while drug trafficking online using the darknet continues to represent only a fraction of drug trafficking as a whole, it continues to grow rapidly, despite successes in shutting down popular trading

platforms" - Yury Fedotov (Executive Director, United Nations Office on Drugs and Crime).

The rate at which this abuse is occurring in Nigeria is not encouraging at all. Some of our youths who abuse drugs are not even afraid of the authorities that kick against this. Some that hid before they smoked marijuana are no longer afraid. Today, they even smoke it in open places and nothing happens. It is a sign of moral decay in the country we find ourselves. Things that are to be afraid of are no longer taken serious. Things have fallen apart and they do as they like.

Sex among students in universities and colleges in Nigeria is seen as normal. The males cling on the females as if that is part of the courses they were sent to the university to study. Almost all the students in the Nigerian universities do not want to walk alone. As a result of this, the males get high in drug in some cases because they want to satisfy their girlfriends during sex. They do this often without considering the adverse effects of what they are getting themselves into.

Some are so addicted to drugs to the extent that they do not have time for their academics. It is all about smoking marijuana and taking of other hard drugs and then sleeps till the next day. The exercise of taking hard drugs continues the next day after they wake up. Some parents think that their children are studying in the universities unknown to them that their children's area of interest had been shifted to how to take drugs and generate gratification. It is sad and many parents do not have the time to pay impromptu visit to their children in colleges and universities.

Some youths in Nigeria die young. Some die through heart attack and others in ghastly motor accidents. Abuse of drugs can result to heart attack. It takes drug abuser unaware. It may come when the youth wants to enjoy his life and take him unknowing that it was the side effect of the drug he abused sometime ago. Also, some of the accidents that occur on roads are because the youths were high after taking drugs. At the influence of hard drugs, they see risk as nothing can run into people and cause casualties. They see things differently when they are high in drugs.

Because of the attitude of some Nigerian youths towards drugs, the upcoming young people have been deceived. Some of them see the life of drug abusers as the best kind of lives one can live. Some have started changing their footsteps to be like hard drug takers, until they leave the care and monitoring of their parents and get to the university, they show in fullness the life they have been dreaming to live. Some believe the university will be a place for their full manifestation because none of their close ones will be there to monitor them.

So many media companies have frown at the rate of drug abuse among the youths in the country. These they made known through publications bearing different titles but all of them point at drug abuse in the country and the bad sides of such. It is not everything that the government of Nigeria will solve for the citizens. To this effect, parents and guardians have to form a team and fight against the abuse of drugs among the youths of the Federal Republic of Nigeria.

Some youths in the country today think that they know more than the experts in a particular field of study. They even see their elders as people that practiced "old school" lifestyle and therefore cannot tell them (the youths) what to do. They prefer to do that which is in their minds and end up blaming themselves in the future. The rate at which the youths abuse drugs is alarming. It gets worse on daily basis. Some see it as nothing and a way of life. They forget that some things that are sweet kills silently.

2.1 What is Drug Abuse?

According to Dr Ananya Mandal of News Medical, drug abuse or substance abuse refers to the use of certain chemicals for the purpose of creating pleasurable effects on the brain. Medical Dictionary defined drug abuse as habitual use of drugs not needed for therapeutic purposes, solely to alter one's mood, affect, or state of consciousness, or to affect a body function unnecessarily (as in laxative abuse).World Health Organisation, WHO, describes drugs and substance abuse as "the harmful or hazardous use of psychoactive substances, including alcohol and illicit drugs (WHO 2017)". According to Medline Plus, Drug abuse also plays a role in many major social problems, such as drugged driving, violence, stress, and child abuse (Medlineplus 2018).

"There are over 190 million drug users around the world and the problem has been increasing at alarming rates, especially among young adults under the age of 30. The 2018 World Drug report released by United Nations Office on Drugs and Crime (UNODC) on 26th June 2018 states that in 2015, there were 450000 deaths that have occurred due to drug use and its complications (UNODC 2018)".

The youths of the Federal Republic of Nigeria have taken substance abuse as a culture. In rural and urban communities of the country, it is common. It is trending and many are not ready to stop it.

"Over fifty percent of youths and women in Kaduna State are into drug abuse, the State Bureau for Substance Abuse Prevention and Treatment has said (Channels TV Report 2016)". In Nigerian universities and institutions of higher learning, abuse of marijuana, tramadol and codeine are everyday practice. These three drugs are the most abused in the country by the youths. It is hard to visit any off-campus hostel in the universities in the country without seeing any student that abuses any of the mentioned drugs. United Nations data reported that Nigeria has the highest level of abuse of cannabis (marijuana) in Africa (2011 Report of United Nations Office on Drugs and Crime). "The number of illicit drugs seized by the National Drug Law Enforcement Agency (NDLEA) stood at a whooping 309, 713kg in 2017 with cannabis and tramadol accounting 90 percent, a report from the National Bureau Statistics (NBS) on drug seizures and arrest statistics says - Business Day News." Because of the abuse of codeine by Nigerians, largely youths of the country between the ages 18-30 years, Federal government of

Nigeria banned the importation of codeine as active pharmaceutical ingredient for cough drugs preparations. The Minister of Health, Professor Isaac Adewole made this known in his office in Abuja on Tuesday, May 1st 2018.

3.2 Effects of Marijuana

Here, we will be looking at the negative effects of Marijuana on youths. Marijuana has many side effects which many youths do not know. Among the side effects of the abuse of the drug are:

Greater chances of being unemployed or not getting good jobs
No good owner of a particular company will like to employ someone who may act in an abnormal way at any point in time. On the other hand, because marijuana is a banned product in the country, no company will be pleased to have his company workers as the offenders of the law. This in one way or the other affects the reputation of the company negatively.

It is good for employers to know the kind of staff they employ in their organizations so as to maintain some level of clean sheet and do not dent their image. On the other hand, drug abuse can reduce a person's employment prospects, both by reducing productivity and by decreasing the chance of getting a job in the first place, especially if an employer tests applicants for illegal drug consumption. –Federal Reserve Bank of ST Louis (Central of America's Economy). Abuse of drug by youths of any country is bad. Youths have to be clean.

Decline in IQ

IQ stands for intelligent quotient. Marijuana is a psychoactive plant. It affects the brain of the consumers. As a result of this, it gradually lowers the IQ of people that "swim" in it. A more recent study published in 2012 suggests that heavy cannabis use during adolescence and teen years can lead to cognitive decline. The research examined 1,037 individuals and followed them from birth to year 38. The researchers found that chronic cannabis consumption over a twenty-year span was associated with a loss of 6 IQ points. There have been students who were doing well in their initial studies but they began to drop in their academic performance since they found themselves into drug abuse. Many dropped out of school because of their poor performance due to drug abuse. Students who were into taking of this weed have narrated their experiences on how it affected their performance in school. Many of them made it open when they were undergoing rehabilitation. Twenty three years old Jasper from Abia State, who was very brilliant back in secondary school started smoking marijuana at age 17, the same year he got admission into the university. Jasper started well in class until he was introduced to smoking cigarette and then marijuana. "At a point I wasn't getting satisfaction from marijuana. That was how I decided to look for substances that will give me a stronger feeling. I then decided to be living on tramadol, rohypnol and codeine," he said. Like the euphoria it gave him, Jasper started missing classes, started spending all his school money on drugs because he needed to maintain the certain level of that 'highness' constantly. Exams came and he couldn't cope until he was advised by the

167

management to withdraw; all within his first year in school.

Severe anxiety, including fear that one is being watched or followed (paranoia)

Sometimes when they smoke cannabis, in their high, they talk as if they can do everything in life. These things happen because the drug has started working in them already. They perceive everything as being simple and common. But immediately it clears from their eyes, fear grips them. Even if they are in their rooms in the night and hear a little step of passerby, they become afraid. That's the effect of the marijuana they were taking. Some of them while walking on the road usually have the feeling that someone was following them. When they turned their back, they do not see anything. At that point in time, the drug they took performed its work on them. This attitude makes the abusers feel uncomfortable.

Increased heart rate (risk of heart attack)

Many youths who think they are big guys and ladies by smoking of

168

marijuana do not know they call heart attack upon themselves gradually. This may not surface immediately but in the long run. It's a drug that increases heart rate which can result to heart attack. According to Harvard Health Publishing of Harvard School of Health, "One of the few things scientists know for sure about marijuana and cardiovascular health is that people with established heart disease who are under stress develop chest pain more quickly if they have been smoking marijuana than they would have otherwise. This is because of complex effects cannabinoids have on the cardiovascular system, including raising resting heart rate, dilating blood vessels, and making the heart pump harder. Research suggests that the risk of heart attack is several times higher in the hour after smoking marijuana than it would be normally".

Nigerian youths should say no to drug abuse. It does much more harm than good. They should not use their money to buy what will kill them one day. Let us be wise in our decisions and actions as youths. Prevention is better than cure so let us desist from consumption of marijuana, codeine, tramadol and other hard drugs that may cause us pain and discomfort.

3.3 Other adverse Effects of Drug Abuse in General

The abuse of drugs globally has many adverse effects unknown to the victims. Sometimes when one try to lecture the abusers to stop as they have a lot of bad sides, the advised sometimes pick it as an offence.

Weakening of the body system

As being said, too much of everything is bad. In the same line, too many taking of drugs is bad. The youth who feels he is a big guy by taking hard drugs is ignorant of the harm he is putting himself into. With time, the result begins to show. The result shows when the fellow has left the youthful stage to adulthood. What he may be able to do ordinarily he finds difficult to do because of the fact that his system has become weak. Sometimes, the weakness of the body system show at the youthful stage as well.

Different types of drugs affect your body in different ways, and the effects associated with drugs can vary from person to person. How a drug effects an individual is dependent on a variety of factors including body size, general health, the amount and strength of the drug, and whether any other drugs are in the system at the same time. It is important to remember that illegal drugs are not controlled substances, and therefore the quality and strength may differ from one batch to another (Better Health Channel 2017).

When the system of the abuser becomes weak, he begins to wonder what the problem may be. What others whom he is in the same bracket can do successful without much stress, he finds difficult to do. That is one of the reasons why some people look older than others whom they are in the same age bracket with.

Why he could not do those things which others could do is because when he was busy drugging himself, other persons were taking healthy food. No one can eat his cake and still have it back. The person who abuses drug at the youthful age should wait for weakness of the system in the future because he or she has eaten all the cakes of healthy living during the youthful age.

Chemicals are bad. Chemicals can degrade the initial standard of a particular commodity when not kept safe. When not used in the appropriate proportion as prescribed by the physicians in the sector, it may cause a lot of harm since the drugs are made of chemicals.

When people keep taking them in large quantity different from the prescription, it gets stored in parts of the human system. As this goes on, it begins to attack the system. With time, the system of the drug abuser is weakened by the chemicals taken long time ago. Some people that suffer from stroke today find themselves in that state as a result of the abuse of drugs. The accumulation of chemicals makes the immune systems to be weak. At this state, they can easily be struck by stroke. This is because their system is porous at that point. Drug abuse weakens immune system, increasing the risk of illness and infection (Gateway Foundation 2018).

Questionable Behaviour

Have you seen where someone that is high in marijuana laugh? Have you noticed how they talk when they are under the influence of marijuana? Everything is usually on a high tone. When they laugh at that state, they laugh like people who are insane. Their behaviour is usually different.

The same thing applies to people that drug themselves using other stimulants. When someone takes alcohol more than the quantity expected, it becomes an abuse. That is to say that the person gets drunk in drinks. When one gets drunk, he behaves in a way he may not behave when in his normal/original state. This will make people see him as irresponsible because he displays questionable behaviour under the influence of alcohol. Drug abuse has really passed wrong messages concerning a particular abuser to the masses. It is not a good thing to get involved because it has the possibility of tarnishing the image of a person.

Drugs affect your body's central nervous system. They affect how you think, feel and behave. The three main types are depressants, hallucinogens and stimulants. **Depressants** slow or 'depress' the function of the central nervous system. **Hallucinogens** distort your sense of reality. **Stimulants** speed or 'stimulate' the central nervous system.

Drugs interfere with the way neurons send, receive, and process signals via neurotransmitters. Some drugs, such as marijuana and heroin, can activate neurons because their chemical structure mimics that of a natural neurotransmitter in the body. This allows the drugs to attach onto and activate the neurons. Although these drugs mimic the brain's own chemicals, they don't activate neurons in the same way as a natural neurotransmitter, and they lead to abnormal messages being sent through the network (NIDA 2018).

As a youth, if you are interested in one political position or the other, you may not be able to achieve the goal if detected that you are a drug abuser. If you are an addict to drugs, that becomes the worse. The reason why you may not get to that political position you desire can be because of the behaviour you are likely to display when under the influence of drugs. Also, you may put the country and the party you are member into trouble by doing things in an abnormal way.

No political party all over the world likes public disgrace. So to avoid that from happening, you can continue with abuse of the drugs you are in love with while the political party selects the candidates they believe are credible and can deliver. They select candidates they know will behave well because he or she is clean from drugs. Drug abuse has painted the images of Nigerian youths black and makes their behaviours questionable.

Loss of self control

If that young man likes to fight, check him very well because something may be pushing him to do so unknowing to you. There may be a propelling force that acts from inside to make him do what he usually does. Any small quarrel he has already turns that into fight. Still check him well because there may be some chemical reactions inside of him that usually cause him to display that way. The chemicals that push him to fight without break can be those from the drugs he usually take. He has no self control.

Abortion is not new in our world today. Such wicked act is seen as everyday routine in the current world we live. "Go and abort that thing because am not ready to father a child now" is what you hear from young male youths who impregnated some ladies out of carelessness. The question is, "why did he not use protection before sex if he must engage in the sex?" Some take such expensive risk because they abused substances and lost control of themselves.

He went to party and took lots of drink and backed up with tramadol when he came back before sleeping with the lady in his room. The lady suggested he wore protection but he said no because he was in a hurry. He was in a hurry to do it and sleep because the drug he abused was seriously working in him.

When it is finally dawn on him that he has impregnated the poor lady, he choose termination of life as an option. Many women in their husband's home today are not able to give birth to children because of the abortion they did when their partner was under the influence of alcohol. Say no to drug abuse and be clean. Being clean will make you calculate effectively before you do certain things.

Aggressiveness

You may not know the evil he is planning in his mind. Show a young drug taker and the author will show you an aggressive youth. Show him that young man in Nigeria that his eyes are always reddish and filled with anger and he will point that marijuana taker to you. They are furious Nigerian youths. They live with drugs and sleep with drugs. They do not get tired of taking different brands of drugs. They are never clean. To be clean is irritating to them. They like and derive great joy in being dirty. To be dirty in this context means to always be high in drugs. They see being dirty always as pride.

The term aggressive is characterized or resulting from aggression. Aggressiveness on the other hand is characterized by or tending toward unproved offensives, attacks, invasions, or the like. What is not supposed to result to quarrel results to that for drug abusers and addicts. We see youths on the streets fighting in hot afternoons over things they do not suppose to fight for. Some on them do such things after taking hard drugs.

Sometimes when you hear the story line on such issue, you will find out that what was causing the fight ordinarily was not suppose to result to what was displayed on the streets. They are little issues that were meant to be settled amicably but they flame them up. The flaming up happened because they were high in drugs. That is one of the adverse effects of drug abuse by the youths witnessed all over the world.

In motor parks in various cities in the country, touts are seen collecting money from bus drivers. They are commonly known as agbero people. Sometimes they charge the drivers more than supposed and are ready to fight at all times when challenged by the drivers. What make their morale to be high always is because of the hard drugs they take. These young men are always filled with aggression. Any little mistake from drivers and sometimes from passengers can result to quarrel. Anger burns inside of them always.

The Mayo Clinic also describes how some stimulants can increase a person's level of aggressiveness. Additionally, discuss the ways of using certain drugs can lead to aggression and violent behaviour. They explained that some substances, such as alcohol, barbiturates and benzodiazepines, decrease a person's anxiety, which in turn makes her more likely to take part in dangerous activities (Foundation Recovery Network 2014).

3.4 Solutions to Drug abuse among Nigerian Youths

The challenge of drug abuse among Nigerian youths can be stopped. But before this fight can be won, the victim of drug abuse has fundament role to play. It may not be easy but it is achievable. If some ideas are taken into consideration, the drug abuser will win at the end.

Rehabilitation

Rehabilitation for years has proven to be one of the key ways to conquer drug abuse among youths. Someone who abuses drugs can become a drug addict. These addicts find it difficult to do without taking of hard drugs in every short interval. To some of them, the drugs they are addicted to are their wives and girlfriends. They are married to drugs.

Rehabilitation is a step-by-step process that helps people to recover. The goal of rehabilitation is to help people function as effectively as possible after a life-changing event. This may include getting them moving again, helping them regain their strength, relearning old skills, or finding new and different ways of doing things.

Base on this section, the rehabilitation we are discussing is how to stop people who are into drug abuse from abusing drugs the more. Many who have been into drugs want to leave the attitude but are finding it very difficult. Rehabilitation will help youths who are addicted to drugs to be free and clean again.

This includes monitoring them and prescribing some diets to them that will make them come out of such pitiable condition with time. Also, drug abusers are taught some things that will make them leave the state of substance abuse of any length. But, rehabilitation is a gradual process. Being free is not a quick thing. Traditionally, substance abuse research and treatment programs have been designed with men in mind, as more men than women typically enter into treatment centers (Treatment Solution 2018).

Self discipline and control

Someone once said that the best advice is the one a person gives to himself. If you want to achieve any target in any area of life, you have to discipline yourself. If you want to build yourself morally, self discipline is what you need to make part of your own self. You build it and nurture it diligently.

In beer parlours, we see youths abusing substances in the name that they want to show they are strong people. How can a young man take 6 bottles of alcoholic drinks in the name that he wants to pride himself that he can drink? Is that not stupidity? He is killing his liver unknown to him. Do not do things because others are doing it. Do not kill yourself by substance abuse because you want to pride yourself as alcoholic drink taker.

Self discipline is what our youths need to stop abusing any form of drugs in any way. Take little quantity of alcohol and save yourself from the problem you may cause yourself in future. Be wise and discipline. If others say that you are not strong by not taking too much, leave them with their thoughts. Let them keep growing with wrong ideology. Time will come when the result of what they called being strong will begin to show on their body. And that may be when they have start advancing in age. Then their body systems become weaker than normal.

The youths have to have control over themselves. They have to train themselves individually. Never allow anybody push you into things you would not like to do ordinarily. That is maturity. You have your life to live.

Since drug abuse and addiction is bad, there is no need to keep swimming in it. You need to hold yourself. You need to control yourself. So many people have vowed that nothing in life will make them addicted to drugs again and they are keeping to the standard till today.

That of Nigeria youths can follow the same trend. Our youths can do it. We can be clean again. If an abuser of drugs picks it upon his self to stop drugs by cultivating self discipline, it is achievable. That behaviour is doable. It can be attained.

Quoting the words of Smart Recovery on self control towards addiction, he stated, "Because everyone has a voice inside his or her head that at least sometimes says, "How about doing something stupid" or, from time to time, a person just feels like doing something stupid – something that works in the moment but not in their life. If you buy the notion that you don't have control over your hands, arms, feet and mouth you are "cooked!" However, when you act consistently with, "Unless I have a stroke, am paralyzed or in a coma, I can always control my hands, arms, feet and mouth," that's exactly what you will be doing and then your beliefs will compel a life without substance abuse or any other form of addictive behavior (Smart Recovery 2012)".

It is in your hands to design the way you want to live your life. If you want to live a healthy life, you can achieve it. And if you want to life a life of mediocre, it is still obtainable. But no one likes to leave in pains for a long time.

Sometimes in life, it is important for one to make some good decisions to shape his or her life better. You have to make the decision to stop abusing drugs. Nigeria youths who abuse drugs need to turn new leaves. It is time to live right. No matter how high a youth may be craving for had drugs, self control and discipline can help him win the battle. Fight and keep your head up. You will win. Nigerian youths can win substance abuse.

Breaking up from peers

Men have done what they would not have done before because of the kind of friends they keep. Some youths were not smoking hard drugs before but they found themselves in that circle because they started keeping friends that smoke. It takes strong self discipline for one not to be influenced to do what the friends are doing. Some attitudes are contagious. People began to do certain kinds of dirty

184

activities because they found themselves in a particular group.

Breaking up from peers that abuse drugs is a solution to drug abuse. It will help a former substance abuser to stay clean. It may not be so easy but it is important to leave.

When one leaves group of drug abusers, he plans his life better. He begins to reason properly as someone who is living in a practical world. Drug abusers most times take things for levity. They most times live their lives like people that have no direction. When they are in their high state, they feel they are in heaven.

Since drug and alcohol users like to spend time with people who share their habits, they may encourage some youths to join in so they have more people to socialize with. The peer pressure that occurs in these settings, and the risky chances youths take to experiment with substances, can be the precursors to a serious and long-term addiction.

If you are a youth that like to keep group friends, ensure you keep those that are clean to some extent. That will make you face less risk of being addicted to drugs. But if you observe that your group friends are advancing in drug abuse, the best is to break up from the chain of such peers. That will make you not be contaminated by the drugs they take. It is better to leave than staying and become dirty in drug.

When you did not know them, you were living. So, breaking up from them will not make you to stop living. If there are things you were gaining from them before, your leaving will make you work more on your own and make it more. It is all about wisdom and doing what is right at the right time.

Youths should not be afraid to leave the bad company they have been keeping. When they observe that what they are seeing is totally different from the way it was before, the best thing to do is to leave. Take bold steps. You have your freedom of choice so do not allow anyone to put you in chains. Do not allow any person influence you negatively. You have your right to take decision of your own.

If someone as a youth have been lured into drugs, he can still leave. There is a solution to win the battle. If the people that make him abuse drugs are his company, he can still solve the problem. And the solution to that is leaving that bad company. Breaking up from peers is a good approach to stop drug abuse.

Anti-drug and anti-addiction education

This is another important approach through which the abuse of drugs among youths in Nigeria and also those in the other parts of the world can be stopped. Some people who are abusing drugs today lack understanding on the danger of what they are doing to themselves. They do not have proper knowledge on the harm they are causing to their entire system. Because of this lack of knowledge, many of them cause failure to their system and live in agony and pains tomorrow.

In November 2009, a Narconon drug educator joined with government officials and educators to bring a drug-free message to the youths in Nigeria. They visited some places where youths are found including secondary schools. In their visit, they educated the young on the benefit of living lives free from drugs. Also, they sensitized the youths on the bad sides of being a drug abuser and the harm such behaviour is likely to cause to the offenders.

School authorities of those schools they visited were happy and commended their efforts in seeing students live clean with clear sense of study. Students articulate when they are free from drugs. They are humbled and listen attentively to the teachings of their teachers when they are clean. But when students take hard drugs before going to their classes, they can be aggressive and cause trouble in the classrooms. Some have quit school because of what drug abuse have done to them. Their heads are always up and never come down. Stubbornness runs in them.

The teaching of anti drug agencies to the youths in the country will go a long way in reducing the chances of youths getting into drugs. When one is educated properly on the risk involved in a particular action he or she wants to take, he may stay away from such action.

If the information says that there is high possibility of death involved in the journey, he quits. Every man loves his life. Even the mad men irrespective of their bad state do not like to die. Life is very expensive.

There are programs held in Nigeria universities every academic section. Programs of this type attract a lot of students both the serious and the non serious ones. It is an avenue to talk to the youths. The anti drug agency of Nigeria can make arrangement with the University managements to address the students on the danger of drug abuse in such programs. Many will learn from such gathering.

National Drug Law Enforcement Agency needs to up their game. They need to work more to reduce youths' involvement in drug abuse. An arm that will educate the youths on the bad sides of drug abuse should be created. The National Drug Law Enforcement Agency (NDLEA) is a Federal agency in Nigeria charged with eliminating the growing, processing, manufacturing, selling, exporting, and trafficking of hard drugs.

With the creation of another sub department of this body that will work specifically in educating the youths to live drug free life, the attitude of the country's youths towards drugs will change. Some Nigerian youth perish because of lack of knowledge and proper education. The places to target for the education of the youths on staying free from drugs should includes churches, schools, sporting centres, and youth groups.

3.5 Drug Abuse in Nigeria Tertiary Institutions

The rate at which the students in tertiary institutions are abusing drugs in Nigerian universities and polytechnics is progressively ascending every year. Both ladies and young men in the institutions all over the country are swimming in drugs. They abuse drugs as if there is no tomorrow. In Delta State University for example, it is hard to see any student hostel free from students that abuse drugs.

According to Coleman Essien's research work on drug abuse

among students in a tertiary institution in the country, among his reports is this "From our findings, it was observed that majority of the drug users were male students although the involvement of females was also evident. Students from wealthy families tend to command the highest number involved in drug use and abuse because of the excess financial allowance given to them by parents.

The participation of students from low income families in drug abuse as observed came as a result of low self-control and social control which can combine to predispose youths to criminality. The studies also revealed an appreciable number of student drug abuser between the age brackets of 20 and 35 years which correspond with the research findings of Obot (1992) that many drug abusers are professionals in their 20's and 30's (Coleman F. Essien 2010).

Irrespective of the fact that youths who are from rich family are the ones that abuse drugs more because of the larger allowances from their rich parents, some of them that are into fraud do abuse drugs a lot. Some of them that are known as yahoo or G boys are into internet scam. They dupe some people to make money. Some due to their passion to advance into scam and make more money, they go fetish. They use their black charm to make their victims pay more money.

Some of these students because they are intoxicated by their riches, look for something that will give them extra joy. In the cause of their search for more happiness, they end up taking hard drugs including cannabis, pakalin, tramadol and the rest. Some of them are so addicted to the extent that they cannot stay a day without abusing drugs.

Moral decay is high in the universities and other tertiary institutions in Nigeria. The youths are not afraid of what could be the outcome of the action they find themselves in the school environment. Sex in the universities in the country is a common thing.

The males are trying to please their girlfriends. They are ready to take hard drugs with the intention to satisfy their girlfriends during sex. They want to last for longer time during sex and that is one of the reasons why some pharmaceutical shops lack tramadol most times. The demand of tramadol from chemist shops is high in the country. The students are seriously buying the drugs to last long in beds without thinking about the side effects of such drug in the long run.

That is the foolishness among the male students in tertiary institutions in Nigeria. They are killing themselves because they want to please a woman that is not their wives. Some of these students after being addicted to tramadol find it difficult to cope without it. Some when they are married began to have issues relating to sexual performance as a result of the harm they have done to themselves when they were in schools due to substance abuse. Substance abuse is bad. It is deadly and not friendly at all.

Many students in universities in Nigeria have abandoned their course of study and pick another course for themselves. Some of them are now studying marijuana also known as 'igbo'. Marijuana has been their course of study since they discovered the silent happiness they derived from it.

Since they discovered their new course, Marijuana, they hardly go to lecture halls to study the initial course given to them when they were writing entrance examinations to be taken into tertiary institutions of their choice. They wake up as early as 5a.m just to grab their lighters and their wraps of marijuana. Some of them after smoking marijuana till 9a.m in the morning go into their rooms to sleep. The wake up after sleep and enter another section of drug abuse.

They wake up later in the day and feel weak and at the end fail to attend the academic lectures which was the reason they were sent to school. In the evening, they gather around to continue with their smoking of marijuana and other drugs. Some of them while smoking their marijuana laugh like mad people in their high state.

Their actions at that point are usually odd.

Addiction to drugs is bad. Some students in tertiary institutions in Nigeria find it difficult to return back to their parents homes at their expected time of their graduation. Because they did not attend lectures as they supposed, they end up having many carryovers. They could not graduate and because of that have to stay back until they clear the courses they failed.

Some of them also do not go home after their graduation because they do not want to leave the bad company they are keeping. They know that they will not have the freedom to continue their drug lifestyle at home. They will be monitored. To avoid the disturbance, some of them who are addicted to drugs pay rent to acquire at least a bedsitter apartment and continue with their substance abuse.

Some of these students continue to abuse drugs without realizing that they have wasted their times in the universities. Some are forced out of the school environment as they could not graduate from their departments. Drugs have done so much harm to the students' abusers of drugs all over the country. The universities in the country are not safe again. Many parents send their children to tertiary institutions to study and some return home dirty in drugs. Parents have to monitor their children closely even when they are still in schools.

Impact of drug abuse on Nigerian students

The impacts of drug abuse on Nigerian students are seen in the following places:

- Poor academic performance

- Crime

- Abusers challenge their teachers

- Dropping out of school

Poor academic performance

Academic excellence is what every student wants to achieve. So many students have that as number one in their scale of preference.

But due to abuse of drugs, their approach towards their studies changes.

The use of hard drugs by adolescent students in Nigerian colleges of education has become an embarrassing occurrence to parents, schools, government authorities, and the society at large. The constant abuse of drugs among this group of students can cause psycho-social problems in society. One may hope that this hateful practice and its associated problems would not lead to the breeding of deranged generation of youths (Muritala&Anyio et al 2015).

This fear is not speculative because of what happens to be the frequent and rampant drug crises in many Nigerian educational institutions. They absorbed new wrong orientation which is quite different from the one given to them by their parents. All these are because of the fact that they are into substance abuse

There was an eye witness of a student that staggered into a

restaurant to eat after smoking shisha in a school in Delta state. He was served 'eba' and soup to eat but when he cut some portion of eba he touches it to the water he was served to wash his hands instead of the soup.

He behaved like someone that was insane before his friend came and rushed him home. He slept for a long time before he woke up the afternoon of the next day.

Imagine a situation whereby the student that displayed the above character has exam the next day. What do you think the student would write? He will not even make it to the examination hall because he would be weak. Even if he makes it, he would not be able to write anything. That means automatic failure for such students.

So many students who abuse drugs in Nigerian secondary schools, colleges, and universities do not do well academically. Their results are usually very poor. Some of them find it difficult to study when they are under the influence of drugs. They are like empty drums that make the largest noise. According to the findings by National Drug Law Enforcement Agency (NDLEA) in 1989, there are significant changes manifested in the behaviour of drugs abusers, and such behaviour include distinct downward performance in school, increased absenteeism, chronic dishonesty, hostility and reduced self-esteem.

Crime

There are students but there are those that are more aggressive than the others due to what they do. They act in different rough ways and they do what other students cannot do in the negative sense. Their fellow students are afraid to talk to them because of how far they have gone into dirty activities.

A normative definition views crime as deviant behaviour that violates prevailing norms – cultural standards prescribing how humans ought to behave normally. Some students behave abnormal after abusing substances. This makes them do what is considered as criminal acts both in the school environment where

199

they study and outside their campuses as well.

70% of the robbery that take place in the universities and other tertiary institutions in Nigeria are carried out by the students. Some of these students that engage in the robbery are students who have taken excess drugs before engaging in their dirty operation. The spirit of fear leaves them when they are high and can break into their fellow students hostels. After their operations, they feel like nothing happened.

Many female students in secondary, colleges and universities are victims of rape. Some who are victims of rape have serious hatred towards their male counterparts and are bitter when approached by male gender for any form of emotional relationship. They pass through trauma in their lives.

Some students who abuse substances are agents of rape. They want to fulfil their sexual desires when they are high and crave for sexual intercourse. At that state, they can force ladies to have sex with them. The ladies in question do not give approval for such act but they do that again at their wish. Some substance abusers are rapists.

Abusers challenge their teachers

Some students who take hard drugs in schools do not respect their teachers. They are ready to fight teachers when they (the teachers) say what they do not like. Some teachers may try to caution these students/drug abusers when they are doing what is wrong and the correction can turn to fight.

Due to their aggressiveness, they are annoyed by little things. They always burn in anger. They may be discussing with their friends while teaching is going in the class, little caution for the uncalled behaviour annoys them. To them, teachers, lecturers or instructors do not have the right to correct them when they do what is wrong.

There are occasions where they challenge their teachers in classrooms and threaten to block them after school dismissal. Some who ended up fulfilling their evil act of beating their teachers after the school dismissal ended up being arrested by

201

policemen by the instructions of the school authorities. Their acts are bad and not justifiable.

An incidence that happened in Anambra State in 2005 had it that a student that smokes marijuana in an abusive manner fought the proprietor of the school when he was trying to discipline him. This made many students of the school abandoned their classrooms and gathered to watch the drama. When the proprietor called the soldiers to come and discipline the students in a hard way. The student (drug abuser) jumped out through the school fence and left.

It is a big blow to many teachers and proprietors that manage schools in Nigeria. Some teachers are even afraid to talk to these students when they enter their classes to teach. Many instructors are careful whenever they enter their classes to teach.

Dropping out of school

What else can they do when their results are nothing to write home about? Where will such students start from? Do they start from their carryover courses of year 1, 2, or 3? Some of them are so many that they dropped out of school.

Some after dropping from school because of what drugs caused them begin to live miserable lives. They feel as if their lives have ended. When they walk on the street, they feel so ashamed because they know people talk bad of them due to their foolishness when they were in school. Some go deeper into smoking of had drugs to forget their worries but that could not solve their problems and worries.

There are still other sides of their drop out from schools. Several school going adolescents experience mental health problem, either temporarily or for a long period of time. Some become insane, maladjusted to school situations and eventually drop out of school. NAFDAC, (2004) as cited by Haladu (2003) explained the term drug abuse as excessive and persistent self-administration of a drug without regard to the medically or culturally accepted patterns.

An insane student cannot articulate in the classroom or lecture halls. The best offer such student can get at that point will be taking him or her to psychiatric hospital where he or she is treated. Some are corrected from the insane while others are not. Before some recovers, they have lost many semesters and hence drop out of school. All these pains are because of substance abuse by students in schools in Nigeria.

Tackling drug abuse in Nigeria tertiary institutions (the author's idea)

This is the constructive view of the author on how to reduce drug abuse in the Nigerian tertiary institutions. It consists of ideas that will help minimize the rate at which drugs are abused in tertiary institutions in the country. If these ideas are considered, there will be drastic reduction in substance abuse.

We see drugs being abused in the tertiary institutions in Nigeria. When you visit some hostels outside the campus, the smell that usually welcomes you from the gate is usually that of marijuana. Some students have taken smoking of marijuana as part of the major courses they take in their schools. Many respect it more than the registered courses they offer in their individual departments. The way they gather and preserve the weeds show that they do not joke with them. Its value is more than that of diamond to them.

Ideas for reducing drug abuse in Nigeria tertiary institutions

The challenge of the abuse of drugs can be reduced to some extent by practicing some good ideas. These ideas are to be properly enforced for effective positive result.

Setting up a group in Nigeria tertiary institutions

It is understood that National Drug Law Enforcement Agency (NDLEA) works to curb the challenge of drug abuse in the country. The fact is that their function is not enough to curb drug abuse in tertiary institutions. A group called **Anti Drug Abuse Agency in Nigeria Tertiary Institutions (ADAANTI)** should be set up in all over tertiary institutions in the country. This group will have a major role to play in the fight against the abuse of drugs among the students of the institutions of higher learning. Also, the

Federal Government should empower and endorse their functions in this area. At the same time, government have to encourage them materially and financially so that they can do their job properly.

The areas this body is to cover include:

Students' examination halls

Some students may be absent during their lectures but not on their examination days. They have to be present in exams as their results are the proof they have to show to their guardians that they attended the school they were sent to. To this effect, ADAANTI has to visit all examination halls on examination days.

In the examination halls, before any is allowed to write, a quick test on drug is run on him or her. Those that test positive for substance abuse are recorded down. The students are allowed to write their exams irrespective of testing positive but actions are taken immediately after their exams.

Through school management, I letter is then written to the parents or guardians whose children or beneficiaries tested positive. The letter will inform the parents and guardians that the young they care for will not be returning home immediately after their examinations. This is to enable team ADAAITI work on them and see how they will correct them from the abuse of drugs.

Rehabilitation centres approach

Addiction is a chronic disease that changes structures in the brain, leading to impulsivity problems and compulsive behaviours, often around intoxicating substances but sometimes around "instant gratification" behaviours like gambling or shopping. The rehab centres of ADAAITI will be an arm of the body that will specifically take care of the students that tested positive on drug abuse. They will work carefully to help the students come out of the bad situation they find themselves. The rehabilitation centres will have good counsellors that will counsel the students and help them out.

The work of the rehabilitation centres will be to focus on therapy and counselling to change behaviours around substances and improve the students understanding of their addiction. This arm will employ experts that are good in that area. It will not just employ people that are academically sound in it but those that are good in therapy and counselling.

Visiting and monitoring hostels

This is another means through which the team will reduce substance abuse in Nigeria tertiary institutions. Some students do not abuse drugs on the streets or inside the school premises. They do that at the comfort of their hostels. The hostels are mainly those that are outside the school campuses.

During the visit and monitoring of these hostels, the group will be assisted by law enforcement agencies like the Nigerian police. The team does not necessarily need go to the hostels wearing their uniforms likewise the members of the police. This is to relieve the students' drug abusers from the fear of being arrested.

During the inspection, any of the students that fall victim of drug abuse will have his or her information taken down. The next is that the group will invite him or her to the rehabilitation centre where he will be monitored and treated properly to come out from the habit of drug abuse.

Visiting chemist and pharmaceutical shops

Irrespective of the fact that some of these drugs that students abuse have been banned by the Federal government of Nigeria, some medical shops still sell them to students. They sell these drugs secretly to the students. They are one of the people flaming up the abuse of drugs among the students and the general public.

ADAAITI will visit medical shops to find out if they still sell such drugs to the students. Also, the student members of ADAAITI will be sent by the body to the shops. They will disguise as if they are drug abusers and demand for these drugs. In the course of the business transaction between them and the sellers, they will take proper record of the discussion between them. They can do that calmly with their mobile phones or any ship that may not be easily detected by the seller. At the end, any of the sellers found guilty

will be punished according to the law. The punishment can involve

closing down of their shops.

References

- Better Health Channel (2017), How Drugs affect your Body, published by Better Health Channel, Victoria, United States

- Coleman F. Essien (2010), DRUG USE AND ABUSE AMONG STUDENTS IN TERTIARY INSTITUTIONS - THE CASE OF FEDERAL UNIVERSITY OF TECHNOLOGY, MINNA, published by Department of General Studies, Federal University of Technology, Minna, Nigeria

- Foundation Recovery Network (2014), Can Drugs make People Violent?, published by Foundation Recovery Network, 1000 Health Park Drive, Building Three, Suite 400Brentwood, TN 37027, United States

- Gateway Foundation (2018), Effects of Drug Abuse and Addiction, published by Gateway Foundation, 55 East

Jackson, Boulevard, Suite 1500 Chicago, IL 60604, United States

- Haladu, A. .A. (2003), Outreach strategies for curbing drug abuse among out-of-school youth in Nigeria: A Challenge for Community Based Organization (CBOS) in A Garba (ed) youth and drug abuse in Nigeria. Strategies for counselling management and control, Nigeria

- Medlineplus (2018), Drug Abuse, published by Medline Plus, U.S. National Library of Medicine 8600 Rockville Pike, Bethesda, MD 20894, United States

- Muritala .I.A et al (2015),Journal of Education and Practice ISSN 2222-288X, Vol.6, No.28, Nigeria

- NAFDAC (2004), A handbook on Prevention of Drugs and Substance Abuse in Nigeria National Drug Law Enforcement Agency, (1989): Stages and effects of drug abuse

- Narconon (2009), Overview of the Drug Addiction Problem in Nigeria, published by Narconon International, 7065 Hollywood Blvd, Los Angeles, CA 90028, United States

- Natasha Tracy (2016), What is Drug Abuse?, Healthy place publication, United States

- NIDA (2018), Drugs, Brains, and Behavior: The Science of Addiction, Published by National Institute on Drug Abuse, United States

- Smart Recovery (2012), Exercising Self Control In Addiction Treatment, published by Self Management And Recovery Training, United States

- Treatment Solution (2018), The Unique Addiction Treatment Needs of Women, published by Treatment Solution, An American Addiction Centers Resource, United States

- UNODC (2018), Women and Drugs: Drug Use, Drug Supply and their Consequences, World Drug Report 2018,

ISBN: 978-92-1-148304-8, Published by Division for Policy Analysis and Public Affairs, United Nations Office on Drugs and Crime, PO Box 500, 1400 Vienna, Austria

- WHO (2017), Substance abuse, published by World Health Organization, WHO Headquarters in Geneva Avenue Appia 20, 1202 Geneva, Switzerland

Chapter 4

Young Fraudsters in Nigeria (Yahoo or G Boys)

The trend in Nigeria for about six years now is the fraudulent activities of G boys also known as yahoo boys. The high quest of Nigeria youths to make money has led them into criminal activities of so many kinds. Both the young and those who are already gaining sense of maturity want to make money either by crook or by hook. It is all about making money by some Nigerian youths irrespective of the source of the money.

Initially, the term Yahoo boy was connected with fraudsters who make money through dishonest means on the internet. There are several proven crooked schemes such people use while striving for immense wealth (Madaily Gist 2018). Yahoo boys in Nigeria are overshadowed with get rich quick syndrome. That is why you can see a young boy of 20 years already wearing very expensive wrist watches, necklaces, and even driving expensive cars.

Nigeria records about N127 billion loss annually to cyber-crime. In 2014 alone, the anti-graft agency – Economic and Financial Crimes Commission, EFCC reported that customers in Nigeria lost about N6 billion to cyber criminals. Banks in Nigeria have lost approximately N159 billion to electronic frauds and cyber-crimes between 2000 and 2013.

According to a report by Ultrascan AGI, a subsidiary of Ultrascan

Research Services – an international research organization, a whopping sum of \$12.7 billion was lost to Nigerian scams (focusing on Advance Fee Fraud statistics) in 2013. In 2012, losses totaled \$10.9 billion from \$9.6 billion in 2011. Another report says that \$50 million is lost annually to romance scams which our brothers participate actively in (OsayimwenOsahon George 2018). Some after falling victim of internet scam by fraudsters ended up committing suicide. Examples of such persons are Marjorie Earl Jones of United States of America and Ian Doney of United Kingdom.

Yahoo Boys are ready to disrespect any elder that try to advise them to stop the fraud they are into. To these young boys, taking advice from any elderly or wise men in their society is making them to be old fashioned. To them, they are current fashioned working with current civilization in the society.

These fraudsters who operate on the internet are making the internet unsafe for the users. They are on social media sites of various kinds. Some of them who are on dating sites claim to be who they are not. Some Nigerian G boys register on dating sites and give themselves fine European and American names. They sometimes make claim like they are Italians living in United Kingdom. They meet foreign women on dating sites and play on their intelligence and at the end dupe them large amount of money. They have many tricks they use.

Some parents who love money irrespective of the source are happy to see their children make money through fraudulent ways. Some fathers are beginning to send their children to experienced scammers in the society to learn how to do scams. All they want is for their children to make money whether the money is clean or not. Some will tell you that there is nothing like clean money. To them, "all die na die". It means that all deaths are death. They are careless about the source of the money.

The pitiable thing is that the G boys in town are going diabolic. It is no longer tricks as usual. Some of them are into rituals. They are ready to make sacrifices of human just to make money. They now kill their fellow humans all in the name that they want to gain power to make money.

That is intellectual poverty that many of them are suffering from. Human life is very expensive but most yahoo boys do not want to hear that. Their hands are soaked in blood. Blood and rituals waste everywhere. Some of them have gone extra mile. They have gone very far to acquire devilish power so that any of their victims they tell to send any amount of money will do that without any questions. They are the young evil men in Nigeria recently. But one thing is sure: there is no peace for the wicked. Souls that they have condemned will come for them.

In this section of this book, we `will be using Yahoo boys, G boys, Yahoo guys, G guys, fraudsters and internet scammers interchangeably. Whenever we use any of these terms just know that we are talking about the same set of persons. They are same persons with so many names because they claim to be smart.

4.1 Confirmed Incidences of G Boys

There are instances of the activities of G boys in Nigeria. Their activities which are bad have been published by news reporting companies. A young man identified as Leeroy Egebe was arrested and arraigned in court by the Economic and Financial Crimes Commission (EFCC) in Warri, Delta state for duping a Swiss woman of N81m. He was arraigned on 8-count charge bordering on conspiracy and obtaining money from a Swiss woman by false pretence (Adunni Amodeni 2018).

Because of the high quest for money, these men do not mind using people they pretend they love for money. This is evident in the news report by a newspaper company in Nigeria whereby a young male student who is an internet fraudster used his girlfriend for ritual. Some of them are into this devilish act so that they can make more money from their victims. Also, some do this to fortify themselves and become richer.

One young G boy used the girlfriend for ritual in early 2018. This was reported by The Guardian News, thus "daughter of the immediate past deputy governor of Ondo State, Alhaji Olugbenga Oluboyo, who was reported missing, Miss Adenike Khadijat, has been found dead in Akure, the state capital. The late Khadijat was found dead under the bed of her Abuja-based boyfriend, Adeyemi Alao, in Oke-Aro area of the city on Thursday, after she was murdered allegedly for money rituals (Oluwaseun Akingboye and Ruth Omasheye 2018)". The lady used by the wicked boyfriend was a 400 level student of Adekunle Ajasin University, Akungba Akoko. Ladies are advised to be careful of the kind of men they have as their boyfriends. All that glitters is not gold.

The most annoying thing is that upon all these evils happening in the society, ladies still follow the young men that they know have no legal jobs to their homes. Why should a lady follow a young man that has no personal legal jobs to their homes? Because of the love for money, many have been killed and some have their virginal fluids cleaned for rituals unknown to them. Ladies should be careful and stop being foolish because of material things they will enjoy for few days and it is over. It is annoying to see ladies with big heads and no wisdom or ability to think well and make right decisions before taking any step.

In the year 2017, Nairaland community reported news on how two Nigerian Yahoo boys scammed Nigerian American businessman. The business man was a Nigerian but does his business in United States of America. The money the two fraudsters duped him in the name that they are land owners was approximately N787million (seven hundred and eighty seven million Nigeria naira).

"A US-based Nigerian businessman was dazed in Lagos, when land agents led him to the lagoon after the part-payment for 150 plots offered for N787.5 million. Kennedy Chukwuemeka Nwabuoku told detectives led by DCP Abutu Yaro, at the Force Criminal Investigations and Intelligence Department (FCIID), Alagbon, how he had paid N577, 590, 792 in instalments among other charges, plus another N18million for bush clearing in February, and how the agents were sending him pictures and videos of caterpillars in action at the purported site at Ifedele Agunbiade village, Sangotedo, in Eti-Osa area of Lagos.

Nwabuoku told the police that he bought the unseen land with a foreign partner and had paid in fiduciary trust, sending monies on different occasions through his company, Ken Bouk Global Investment Ltd. Identified as Emeka Okoronkwo and Michael Owolabi Alonge, the agents, according to Nwabuoku, had offered the land for sale at N5, 250, 000 per plot with Certificate of Occupancy (Ahamefuna 2017)". These yahoo boys are so tricky to the extent that they can open business accounts with unique names. They are smart but some of them have been caught irrespective of their smartness.

Their smartness makes their works appear to be real but they are faked. Most people fall prey to them because of the level of their packaging. Many people are victims because of their mindsets that it is a company and not individual accounts that they paid to. Some people who they duped paid into the company accounts they created and today the victims cannot see what they paid for. That is the game and that is why they are called G boys.

Nothing can be compared with human life. What is bad is bad. A criminal act is a criminal act and nothing can change that. Also, a wicked act is a wicked and no amount of "baptism" can change it from being what it is. Whether they baptize them G boys, Yahoo boys or Yahoo plus, they are all internet scammers.

The most painful wicked activity of G boys in the year 2018 in Nigeria was the one that happened in Delta State University, Abraka. The wickedness of these young men shook the entire city of Abraka and the country at large. Till tomorrow, the community will not forget that pain.

That was the kidnap and killing of a bright female student of the department of Mass Communication of the university. The student though in 300 level maintained First Class grade. That was a distinction. Irrespective of the great brain possessed by this student who name was Elozino Ogege, the yahoo boys kidnapped and killed her for ritual. Elizino was loved by all. She was dedicated to her studies, respectful, accommodating and always ready to teach her fellow students.

From the report from Vanguard News on November 19, 2018, the company wrote in these sentences:

"The discovery of the late student happened on the same day residents of Umono Street in Abraka, Ethiope East Local Government Area of Delta State discovered the lifeless body of a two-year-old male child abandoned near an electricity transformer. The student, Elozino Ogege, had been declared missing after she was said to have gone out to meet an agent who was assisting her secure an apartment for her with plans of relocating to another part of the university town.

Sources in the area who identified the victim, told Vanguard that she was a 300 level student of the Department of Mass Communication. One of the sources, who simply gave his name as Michael, said: "Her decomposing corpse was found on Friday with

225

her tongue and breast severed from her body (Perez Brisibe 2018)". The Yahoo boys who are coded ritualists used the bright lady by cutting away her breast and tongue.

They drive flashy cars round the town and little do their fellow students know that some of them have soiled their hands in human blood. They are evil blood suckers that fulfil their evil plans in the dark. They are evil boys.

4.2 Terms used by Yahoo boys

Clients

Clients to yahoo boys are people who are victims of their scam. Also, clients can imply some people they are working on to succumb to their scam tricks. You hear them make statements like "my client from United States of America did not pay well this time around". Again, they make statement like "how I wish this my client will pay up to six thousand dollars ($6,000)". Those that have buoyant clients live well because they (the clients) always send money to them in Nigeria from United States or other developed countries.

Voltage

This means how rich a particular person is. A person whose voltage is high is someone who has much money. When a yahoo boy tells you that that his client has a full voltage, what it implies is that the client has much money. The money made by the foreign client can be because he or she does a good job.

Level

It is a slang used by yahoo boys which can mean anything. Outside G guys, it is used commonly by people in different cities of the country. Maybe a yahoo guy told his friend who is into same scam that he is expecting money from a client, later when they meet, the friend may ask how was the level? Meaning how did the business go?

Bomb

Bomb as a term used by internet scammers in Nigeria can mean hack or to hack. When a Yahoo boy says that he is bombing, what it means is that he is hacking. When he says he is searching for a Facebook account to bomb what it means is that he is searching for a Facebook account to hack. When they bomb any of users Facebook accounts, they take over the accounts to carryout their scam.

Mugu

Mugu is a Nigerian word for those who fall victim to Yahoo boys' trick. It implies a fool as well. Also, it is used generally in the country as those who are not wise. Also, the term "mugu" can mean to fall sheepishly to something. Example of the sentence that involves the use of this term is "do you know that the mugu still paid extra five hundred dollars thinking that I am real" Another is "do you know that guy falls mugu to that lady? "

Maga

The term maga implies the person that falls to the scam of the Yahoo boys. It is similar to mugu. It is used interchangeably with

228

mugu. As someone who stays in the environment filled with these scammers, you hear them make sentence like "has the maga pay?" What it means whether the person they planned to scam has paid any money. Maga is the derogatory term used to refer to a foreigner that fall victim to internet fraud schemes of Nigerian fraudsters. These scammers sometimes speak in codes so that a novice will not understand their plans.

4.3 Tricks used by Young Nigerian Internet Fraudsters

They have many ways through which they trap their victims. If they apply plan A and it does not work, they apply plan B and C. But no matter the approach these Yahoo boys use, you cannot fall prey to them if you are careful and up to date. It is important to get information on what is happening in your society every point in time. Also, foreigners have to be wise on their own to prevent being used as Automated Teller Machine (ATM) by these young scammers.

Operation on Social Media sites

They sign up on social media sites with false identity. They sign up on Twitter for example bearing the names of celebrities. They usually do this using the names of foreign artists and actors that are well known.

At first, they try to follow some persons from Europe and United States of America. They may follow about ten thousand white people. After some time, the persons they followed initially on twitter follow them back. Not all will follow but at least reasonable number of persons. Their target is usually people abroad and also those who are working.

When the internet fraudsters who pretends to be someone also observed that some persons they followed before have followed them back, they, the fraudsters, hiding under the image of celebrities go and unfollow others. Doing this make them have more followers. In this case, they have more followers than the people they follow.

At that point, they began to make their intelligent plans for those they will defraud. They began to build webs in which they will use to trap their victims. A scammer who set up a twitter of a Canadian singer Justin Drew Bieber for example follows the activities of the singer properly. If he is to go for a show, the scammer makes an earlier update on that. When he performs in the show, the scammer also showcases that on twitter handle as well. With time, people begin to believe that he is the real Justin Drew Bieber.

Everything looks real but it is all scam. The fraudster just acquired the identity of the real artist. He impersonates the real artists and makes the whole thing looks real. With time, he begins to penetrate the followers.

He may start by twitting that he has a project he is planning to start. He tells the followers that the project is a multi million dollars business. He goes ahead and persuades the followers to invest in the project that after a month of completion of the project, every investor will be paid back with increase of about 200% of their invested capital. Yahoo boys can paint pictures and make every of their plans look attractive and colourful.

When they capture the attention of some of the followers, the business becomes half done. The scammer presents his account details to those that are ready to invest into the project that he claimed. As time goes on, he updates the victims of the progress in the proposed project. The victims believe that everything is real but little do they know that they have been duped by a scammer who lives in one city in Nigeria. He may screen grab beautiful pictures of an ongoing project in a place and upload it to the victims to show them the progress. Also, they sometimes source for pictures from different websites.

When the time he initially told his victims that the project will be completed has come, he may cook another story telling them that everything did not work as planned. He persuades them to invest more and that the return they will get at the end will be much higher. Some of them still pay into the account given to them by the G boy that pretends to be the artist. The young man goes to the bank and withdraws the money and continues to live large while the fooled are hoping that they will get huge return at the right.

At the end when the claimed artist is expected to pay his investors, he backs off. He blocks those whom he scammed on the twitter social media site. Sometimes, they send messages to the victims saying "you have just been duped by a black man". But some of the scammers after duping their clients blocks them on twitter and even delete their own accounts.

The victims regret for their entire life after being scammed of huge amount of money. They cry in silence and curse the person that duped them. They made big mistake they never believed they would. G boys live expensive lives while the victims are in agony.

Sometimes, they hack into the twitter accounts of prominent people and extort money from the friends. So many twitter users have lost a lot of money through twitter by falling prey to the users. It is sad to hear that the social media site is not safe any longer. It hurts many people in our society today.

Yahoo Boys scam through Facebook

Facebook is another social media site that G boys use to defraud users. One of the ways through which they do this is by creating facebook accounts with fake details. They have so many ways they use to dupe people on Facebook.

They can create the account with fake information. A yahoo boy may use the name of a lady and pretends to be the person on the profile picture. He may go and source the pictures of a porn star. He shows the nudity of the lady he is impersonating on his walls pretending to be woman that can always give her body to any man for sex.

He then send friends request to many Facebook users. Some of the users that receive the request accept. Men are moved by what they see with their eyes and because of this many quickly accept the request once they see the exposed body. Some who are aware of their tricks after checking on the profile picture of the scammer

234

declines the request. But those that accept with the mindset that the request was sent to them by a lady that is ready to have sweet sex with them in the long run put themselves in great danger.

The 'sexy lady' in disguise then begins to chat with the Facebook friends. At first she introduces herself as a particular person (note that sometimes it is a man but pretends to be woman, so understand when we use 'she'). She then begins to tell the prospective victim how sexy she is and how she can be so naughty in bed. At the end, she may tell the man that she will like to visit so that they can have fun at night. Some of them pretend to be students that have time for visit during the weekend.

If she is able to capture the attention of thee man by making the man lusty, she is close to achieving her aim which is defrauding the man of money. Some of these G boys capture the attention of their victims by sending them pornographic pictures of the woman they pretend to be. Also, some of them send short videos of where they are fingering themselves and appears to be so naughty.

The next step after capturing the attention of the victim by making the man to be emotionally high is to demand for the transport fare she will use to come down. The young man pretending to be a hot lady may tell the man that 'she' is coming from a far place. The essence is because 'she' wants to make good amount of money from the man.

The man demands for 'her' account number and it was sent. 'She' may send an account number bearing another lady's name and tell the man to pay in that 'her' own account is dormant. They can cook stories that appear to be real. That is what makes them scammers.

After the transport money has been sent, the next demand can be money to buy clothes to wear for the visit. 'She' may tell the man that all her clothes are old. When succeeded in convincing the man for the money for clothes and then sent again, she promises the man that she will be coming next weekend.

The heart of the man gladdens and he keeps preparing for the unknown lady that will arrive in the next weekend for them to have great sex. But little did he know that the person he had been chatting with is a man pretending to be a woman. When the faithful day for the appointment comes, the lady will not show up. The man chats with the lady asking for explanation and she gives an excuse.

At this point 'she' may tell the man that she had accident. All is the tricks they work with. After excuses upon excuses, the victim becomes tired. After much pressure from the man, the scammer may block the man and there will be no conversation between them again. The money the man sent is gone. That is Nigerian G boys for you. They can play on people's emotions. Some of them are good at that.

Another way through which these bad guys scam people on Facebook is by hacking into the users account. They have been doing this and have been succeeding for years now. It is advised that everyone that does not want to have his or her Facebook account hacked should use strong password. Also, it is not advisable to login into your Facebook accounts using public computer, for example logging in through computers used in Cyber Café.

Internet scammers can lay their hands on the same computer you just finished making use of and changed your password unknown to you if you did not log out before you left. And sometimes your browsing time expires why browsing at Cyber Café and you could not log out before you leave. You consider the money you will spend in buying another time and you decide to leave.

Some people wake up in the morning and tried logging in to their Facebook accounts but could not do that. What is the meaning of this? What really happened? I cannot login again but I know my password. Sorry, someone somewhere has acquired your Facebook account. It is gone. Someone else has taken control and that is a G guy that may come from Nigeria. It is their job. They hunt for accounts to hack every blessed day.

Do not use your phone number as your password on Facebook.

That is how they acquired so many accounts of the users of the social media. Some people use their phone numbers as their passwords for easy remembrance but it is not healthy. Your Facebook account can easily get hacked when you adopt such approach. Your password should be mixture of alphabet, numbers, and special characters. This will make it difficult for yahoo guys to hack your Facebook account.

Also, the use of your date of birth as password is risky as well. It makes your account vulnerable for internet scammers to penetrate. It should be elements that their minds will be difficult to get.

When the internet fraudsters take control of the account of an active user, they can go far in getting what they need. They first go through the messages of the person they hacked the account. This makes them to discover the persons' the user chats always. Their next step becomes money demands. They may send messages to one of the major persons demanding for money and to pay back within certain intervals.

When the person did not confirm by calling the person that demands and sends the requested amount, the scammer goes and withdraw the money. He may frame a story that he was in a particular place and should send the money to another person's account. But the victim may not know that the account number given to him was the impersonator account number. He still meets others by sending messages requesting for monetary assistance. Other people send the money with the mindset that their friend is in need.

Before many discovered that they were scammed that the account of their friend was impersonated by a fraudster, it had already become late. The scammer had already made good amount of money from them before his victims found out. Yahoo boys are threat to Facebook social media today.

Some of these fraudsters adopt the approach of creating groups on Facebook and claim that the groups are non-governmental organizations. They claim that the groups are located in a particular region in a country. Some may say that a non-governmental organization located in Oakland in United States of America with a particular name is taking care of some people who are suffering from serious sickness. They go further by saying that the members of the group need to donate money even as small as 20 dollars to save the dying.

The G boys/guys paint the picture of the whole thing as if it is real but it is not. They regularly upload the pictures of those they claim are dying and need financial assistance. Those who are ignorant of the activities of these scammers fall prey to their packaged story.

Take for example that among two thousand members of the group, that 800 persons donates 20 dollars each, that is a good amount of money. If you multiply 800 by 20 dollars, it will give a total amount of 16,000 dollars. That is total of sixteen thousand US dollars. If the G guy is from Nigeria, the young man made approximately 5.7 million naira from the scam. That's a dubious act that makes them spend money lavishly. Beware of Yahoo boys from Nigeria. Confirm any information you see on Facebook as well as other social media sites.

The rate of moral decay in Federal Republic of Nigeria is very high. So many Nigerians takes the things of God for levity. Some of these young fraudsters have claimed to be pastors or priests of churches in Nigeria just to dupe people good amount of money. That is devilish.

A powerful and famous Catholic priest Rev. Fr Ejike Mbaka has been impersonated by the G guys on social media, particularly Facebook and these wicked souls have dupe Nigerians home and abroad using the name of the man of God. When this crime got to the ear of Fr. Mbaka, he voiced that he was not the one. He said that he was not on Facebook and those who used his name for such atrocity will suffer unless they repent. As of the time of publication of this work, Rev. Fr. Ejike Mbaka of Adoration Ministry Enugu has no Facebook account of any kind.

In the year 2018, it was gathered that Reverend Father Ejike

Mbaka caught one of the fraudsters who have been using his name to scam people. The report shows that the young man was an ex-seminarian. It was painful to hear that.

"The Spiritual Director, Adoration Ministry, Enugu Nigeria, Rev. Fr. EjikeMbaka has exposed a man who has allegedly been using his name to scam people. It was gathered that the man, an ex-seminarian, hails from Imo State. The ex-seminarian has been scamming people in Awka with Father Mbaka's name until he was caught. In a video, Mbaka, however, brought the man to his Adoration Ministry Enugu ground and exposed him completely in front of the congregation (Don Silas 2018)".

This is for someone who impersonated him physically. There are many who has impersonated him online including Facebook and have not been caught till date. They are intelligent Yahoo guys.

Nigerian Youth Scammers on Dating Sites

It is their jobs. They are good at it. They have duped many people and are still going to dupe more for thousands of dollars. They go into dating sites searching for working white ladies they will scam to make money. The category of white women that fall victim are those who are adults but still need men to stay with. Some of them are those who were divorced. Some of them are advanced women but want to satisfy their sexual desires and others need men to answer their names. They want to get married.

These young men can be in Nigeria and still have foreign phone numbers. They paid for these phone numbers to the telecommunication companies in United States and other foreign countries and have the ability to use them here in Nigeria. When you call them on the foreign numbers they answer and communicate well with you.

So, do not be surprised if they give foreign number and you call and communicated with them. Also, some of them have voice changing applications installed in their phones. If they pretend to be women and the men who are victims call them, they speak like women to the men with the help of the voice changing application installed in their phones.

Nigerian G boys enter dating sites claiming who they are not just because they want to make money in a dubious way. Some claim to be Italians working in United Kingdom while others claim something else. They paint good pictures of who they claim to be. What is important to them is that they make their money at the end.

After being friends with the women they want to scam, they began to discuss. Their first approach is to know what the women do. This will make them to find out if the women can give them the amount of money they need in the long run. The reason is because they must make attempt to scam the prospect. That is their main reason for being on the site.

As days goes on, they began to go deeper into erotic chat. They can go into sex chat with the women they pretend to love. This makes their prospect feel horny and their attention captured.

The criminals who are the G boys in this context go deeper and deeper. They do not mind dropping their nude photos to the women every early morning. This makes the women feel that their 'men' love them so much. They have been captured emotionally if the clients begins to feel this way.

With time, the G guy may tell the 'lover' that he was not feeling well and that he needed about one thousand dollars for treatment. The woman began to source for money because she needed to save the lover who is a coded Yahoo guy. In this state, the guy speaks as if he is really sick. He knows his job.

She gets the money and sends to him. The woman who did that had in mind that her lover would come and marry her when everything is in place. The G boy continues to extort money from the victim he got online. The scam continues until the woman realizes herself and stops sending money to him.

To show you how powerful these Yahoo boys are; some of them can control the women to leave their home countries to Nigeria just for them to come and see these fake lovers. There are such incidences. When they come, they lodge in hotels making love with their fake lovers until they go back to their home countries. What make the women to come down to see their "lovers" is usually because they have waited for a long time without seeing their "lovers" in real life and touching them. They want to feel them through sexual contact and be happy.

How G boys scam people as investors and project executors

They have many ways they adopt to dupe people. Some of them claim to be investors and encourage others to invest with them claiming they will pay back with mouth watering interests. It is completely faked. They are not real. They just want to go away with your hard earned money.

Investing can be a minefield for beginners and experienced traders alike. Not only do beginners have to learn new financial instruments and trading lingo, but they also have to be on guard against the slew of scammers and fraudsters seeking to prey on novice traders. Similarly experienced traders can become victims because as their confidence becomes complacency (Lawrence

247

Pines 2018).

Nigerian internet fraudsters set up brokers sites claiming to be real and searching for investors. They sometimes go into online communities in search for some foreigners who are well to do and need ways to maximize their profits. When they meet these clients, they confuse them by telling them that they have ongoing projects that need investors. They can tell their 'preys' that if they are able to invest in a particular country, they have high return in terms of interest within the next 20 days.

For example, a Nigerian G guy can tell his client that if he invests in United States, he will get the invested money with interest of 20% within 20 days. But if the investor invests in Nigeria, he will get the capital with interest of about 120% within 20 days. That is the trick.

Because everyone likes interest, he decides to invest in Nigeria. But do you know the trick behind the game? The reason why the scammer gives higher interest for Nigeria is because he can easily

248

pick the money in the country. There will no stress. But if the investor chooses to invest in a country like United States, he may not make much gain. The thing is that when the victim sends the money to United States, the fraudster has to look for someone that will receive the money over there in United States of America for him. And the person who receives the money is paid some percentages as he sends the money down to the Yahoo boy in Nigeria after picking the money through Western Union, MoneyGram or through any other channel.

That is how the scam goes on. When it is time for the scammer to pay the defrauded, he cooks a sweet story for the victim. Some of them delete their account from the site after scamming two or three persons. The money becomes lost and not traced.

Worldwide $16 billion was lost to various types of fraud, scams and identity theft in 2016. This represents a 16% increase over 2015 and is the highest level of fraud recorded since Javelin Strategy & Research (the firm behind the report) began tracking this statistic in 2004. Fraud affects every region of the globe and manifests itself in many different forms (ibid).

These Yahoo boys are bad boys. Another way through which they scam people online is through Binary. They search for investors as well here. They work tirelessly day and night sourcing for ways to make money. These young Nigerian men think far to get their jobs done in intelligent ways. Some of them are technologically sound.

A binary option is a financial exotic option in which the payoff is either some fixed monetary amount or nothing at all. Binary has been corrupted by Nigerian youths who are scammers. Many binary option outlets have been exposed as fraudulent (Federal Bureau of Investigation). The U.S. FBI is investigating binary option scams throughout the world, and the Israeli police have tied the industry to criminal syndicates.

Nigerian youths are into binary but their aim for going into that is to scam people. They do go into that not to do clean business but to dupe investors and run away. They have sugar coated tongues but are coded criminals. Their hands are not clean at all.

When they meet investors, they persuade them to invest in a particular project and get mouth watering interest within a certain period of time. They send the details of payment to the investor and he sends the money down to Nigeria. The young fraudster bounces into Nigerian bank and pick up the money through any abroad money receiving channels.

When the agreed time for the investor to receive the capital and the interest for the investment has reached, the investor receives an alert that a particular amount of money has been credited to his account/wallet. This alert is engineered by the Nigerian scammer. The client logs in and sees the money. But for him to collect the money and spend he could not. It looks surprising to him (the victim).

He walks into the bank to complain of the issue and the bank tells him that the fault is not from them but from the broker (the sender of the money). The duped writes back to the 'scammer' pretending to be a broker. The "broker" tell him that he needs to pay for signal for the money to be accessible by him. These bad guys sometimes put fear in their victims by telling them that if they don't pay, the money they have invested will be lost.

They are wicked souls that have no human sympathy. Because the investor do not want to loose the huge amount of money he has invested, he goes and pay for the so called "signal". There is nothing like "signal" payment but the scammer did that to steal more money from the victim. After payment, the scammer confirms the transaction. Now he may send few amounts of dollars that his 'prey' can have access to. He gets bank alert on that and feels that everything will take shape with time. He makes attempt to withdraw the money and it works. But he has not yet been able to have access to the main good amount of money. The money is not yet accessible.

The victim writes back that he received the one sent but not yet able to access the first money sent to him which includes the main capital and the interest. The G guy apologizes and tells him that the technicians are still working on the issue that he would have access to all his money soon. Coded criminal in quote is the G boy.

After few days, the scammer writes back to the investor telling him that he has to pay for Access as soon as possible. He may add fire to the duped foreigner that everything will be lost if he does not act fast. It's a pity. Men playing on the intelligence of others are bad men.

The victim does everything possible to make sure that he meets up. He gathers the money and makes the transfer expecting everything will work out finally. Once the victim sends the money, the fraudster goes to the bank and withdraws the money.

The next is that he goes to the site and deprives the victim access to the site. The victim of the binary scam would not have access to the site again not to talk of communicating with the scammer again. That is the wickedness among Nigerian young scammers. It is evil. Someone is somewhere enjoying another man's money and the duped cries bitterly. Man's inhumanity to man.

You have to be careful on how you believe things you see online in order to be safe. Do not register on every website you see. Some of them are there to get your personal details. Verify to know the authenticity of the site. Some that you meet online and they tell you they are looking for investors or are searching for investors are fake people. They are not real. They are searching for who they will defraud.

Bitcoin which is the trending is becoming faked. Yahoo boys are defrauding many people through this channel. They know how to manipulate some people. They are good manipulators. They tell you they have Bitcoin to sell that you should credit them. Once you credit them in dollars, they block you and you lose your money. You cannot get the Bitcoin equivalent of the dollars you paid to them.

ATM card hack (Local Operation) by G boys

They rush into the bank crying. They cried to the customer care section of the bank complaining of what happened to them. Some of them are students while others are old women who cannot read or write. They were pitied by the staff of the bank. But at the end, nothing could be done for the recovery of the money. The customers have lost their hard earned money to Nigeria young scammers. Some are being told of the process to pass through which among them is reporting to police station to know if they could get their money back but many are afraid of going to the police to report. The security sector of Nigeria is messed up, so some victims of local scam see going to police stations to report as means of losing more money.

So many people are in fear because of the actions of these young criminals. When the customers who were duped by them are crying, they, the scammers, are somewhere already partying with the money they stole from poor women and men in the country.

Tell me how nemesis will not catch up with the criminals. After stealing from poor people in the country intentionally, you come out calling yourself a big guy. A criminal is a criminal and that is what they are.

The worst is that some of these people they dupe are helpless students whom their parents struggled hard to gather the money and sent across to them for school fees. And a coded young man who calls himself a yahoo boy use tricks to steal. There are so many things God will judge; criminals being happy at the bitterness of other people.

Many Nigerians are even afraid to have their money in the bank as a result of the rate of scam going on in the country. Many of our youths do not want to work again. What they want is hot money. And the funny thing is that they do not know some of this hot money kills.

One of the ways they scam people locally in the country is by sending messages to account holders in the banks telling them that their accounts have been blocked. Some of them read that the ATM card has been blocked. Some send text messages using the bank's title telling their prospects that their BVN is blocked. They further persuade the receiver of the message to call a particular number. It is a common scam carried out by the young scammers in Nigeria.

They have a unique way of constructing the scam messages. An example of the message they use to scam people reads thus: "Dear Customer, due to the BVN validation in compliance with CBN directives, your ATM card has been deactivated. Call our helpline on 08034138959 now".

Once the receiver of the message calls and follows the instructions given to him by the coded criminal, the money in his account gets debited within few minutes. When the receiver calls the phone number he is instructed to call, the person pretending to be a customer care agent calls his name. This makes the prospective victim to believe that the person he called was a customer care agent of the bank.

The prospective victim of local scam will be like "since this young man called my name, he will be from the bank for sure. But little did he know that someone that knows him maybe the person that supplied his full name to the scammer. Also, there are applications that can detect peoples' names which many people are not aware of. That is the game. That is the scam. The fraudster pretending to be an agent of the bank asks the receiver of the message few questions including the last time he used his ATM card.

When the man supply the information the scammer needs, he smiles that he is making headway in the criminal trick. He is further asked to call out his card number and the ATM card pin. If he does that, the work of the scammers are almost done. The scammer tells the prospective victim of the scam that a five digits pin will be sent to him to fasten the activation process and once that is done that he should send him the pin.

Immediately that pin is sent to him and he sends it or calls it to the hearing of the scammer, he turns from prospective victim to full victim. At this point, the money of the victim becomes debited from his account. What the scammers did was that they installed mobile application on the phones they "use for their businesses" and then transfer the customer's money to another account of their choice. Many Nigerians are victims of this kind of fraud. Some Mobile Applications can transfer maximum of one million naira in a day in Nigerian banks.

In Nigeria, many businesses have fold because many Nigerians are victim of this kind of fraud. Some loss the money they use for their businesses to these wicked souls that call themselves Yahoo boys. They are big time criminals. They take advantage of people that are not informed.

Since this kind of scam became rampant in the country, banks have been sending notifications to customers not to disclose their card numbers and pins to people. Irrespective of the notifications, many are still falling victims. Some who cannot read and have account numbers are still victims to the challenge. It is a big challenge in the country. Some who can read are always in a hurry to read through short messages sent to them by their individual banks. Even when some are in banks and the staffs want to educate them on important information, many do not pay attention because they are always in a hurry to go.

G Boys Hack into Bank Customers Account

This kind of hack is highly technical. These bad boys have grown to the level of hacking into accounts of bank customers. It is difficult to know if these boys have insider in the banks that help them carryout this kind of bad action or they have applications that are so rugged to break into some customers account.

In this kind of fraud by G guys, they target rich men in the society. They do this because they know they will make good amount of money if they succeed in doing so. It is a risky stealing. It is risky in the sense that if they are caught they will end their lives in prisons.

When these criminals have access into customers account, their first move is to change certain information in the account. These include the original phone number and email address of the account holders. Sometimes, they deactivate them so that the owner of the account will not receive any alert or notifications on what goes on in their accounts.

Gradually, they begin to move the money in the victim accounts to their own accounts. Also, sometimes they move the money to their friend accounts or to accounts of people they have met before. They may call someone for his account number so that they can empty the accounts of their victims.

It is advised that customers should not give their account details to people they do not know too well. Even if you know the person as a scammer, never give your account details to him or her. It is risky to do that. The reason is that they may put you into trouble.

If you give your account number to scammers or people you do not know, they may make transfer of money obtained through dubious way to your account. When this happens, you may not know. Your bank account may be monitored until you go to the bank to withdraw money.

At that point when you want to make withdrawal without knowing that your account is monitored, security officials will come and arrest you. You pass through stress for what you do not know much about. Being a financial crime, you may be imprisoned. Until you are able to provide the G guy that hacked the customer's account and made the transfer to you, you will not be released. Suffering for another person's bad action is bad but the bank cannot help until you provide the scammer. It is usually painful.

Another approach that Yahoo boys used to hack into bank customers account was published by The Guardian Newspaper Company in the year 2017. The narration given by the newspaper company showed that some yahoo boys are computer experts. They are technically sound in their operation. The company through the write-up of Samson stated:

"They work in multiple ways, such as sending mails to victims, local or international, purportedly from banks, persuading them to enrol on an offer that would ultimately grant the fraudsters access to hack into the victim's accounts.

At this stage, the victim receives a link purportedly from the bank that automatically redirects to the Internet banking portal, where the fraudsters clone the webpage, despite the fact that banks are not supposed to have access to a customer's Internet banking password.

The fraudster is aware whenever the link is opened and every information entered is seen and watched backend. The scammer then opens the victim's bank authentic Internet banking platform and keys in the username and password entered to login, initiate an Internet banking transfer and waits for the OTP (one time password) to complete it.

At the point when the victim types in his or her OTP on the cloned website, the fraudster completes the first transfer immediately. If the victim doesn't get an alert of the debit, the scammer initiates another transfer and waits for the victim to enter another OTP and then completes the second transfer (The Guardian news 2017)".

4.4 How to avoid being an Internet Fraudster (Young Fraudster)

Some people who are into scam today were not there before. Something pushed them into it and they are tagged scammers today. Everyone wants to make quick money. Everyone wants to live good when there is availability of money. If you want to avoid being a Yahoo boy, there are some qualities and virtues you have to possess. They include contentedness, self discipline, patience, self confidence, mindfulness of groups, and avoiding envy.

Contentedness

What is contentedness? The term contentedness means to be satisfied with things as they are. It is to be satisfied with the things you have right now as you hope for better tomorrow. The youths in Nigeria and those abroad need to have it.

They need to possess it to live at peace. When a youth is not contented with the properties and what he has, he begins to look for alternatives on how to make money either by crook or by hook. Because of this, he may find himself in the midst of scammers in his society. But when you are satisfied with where you are today, you have no reason for being a scammer because of money.

Youths should learn how to be happy in their current stage in life. They have to thank their Maker for making them who they are today. They have to show sign of gratitude. When you are happy with yourself, you do not need to be moved to do dirty things because of money.

Self discipline

If you are well disciplined in life, you will not be moved when you see some fraudulent actions people take to make money. Self discipline will make you see these young fraudsters in your country as people who do not know what they are doing. You perceive them as people who are senseless because what goes around comes around.

This is because when one dupes someone whom he feels is a novice to make money, in one way or the other, he will still spend the money. Again, there will be a point the scammer will get in life, he feels bitter of the bad things he did in the past. He will not have rest of mind. And when you are discipline, you stick on what is right and always do it well. Self discipline brings self respect. When you respect yourself, you do not do things that will make people disrespect you. A scammer is not respected.

Mindfulness of Groups

It is not all groups that worth being a member of. There are some groups you do not need to be a partaker of irrespective of how attractive the group may appear to be. There is a saying that bad company corrupts good manner. This saying is true because if rotten fruits are in contact with the good ones for a long time, at a point the bacteria that attacks the bad ones gets transferred to attack the good ones.

If you do not want to be initiated into the group of Yahoo boys in Nigeria, avoid their group. Also, you have to avoid being a member of groups that have Yahoo boys as part of them. When you associate with the group consisting of their members, when they discuss money and begin to call big amounts of money that they made through their scam, you can be tempted to join them. The amount of money you heard them calling may keep ringing in your brain until you start to ask them how they do it.

It takes strong discipline for you not to ask them. But if you are strongly moved to ask them how they make their money, they can teach you their tricks. When they teach you their dubious ways of making money and they sink into your brain joined with you practicing it, automatically you become a G guy. Everyone begins to see you as one of the young men that use dubious ways to make money from people.

Yahoo boys can be intimidating. If you start comparing their wealth with yours, you may quit the legal job you are doing. You do not need to rub shoulders with any of them because stolen money is stolen money. Such money comes in large amount. So, avoid their company or group so that you are not enticed to become a member overnight.

Avoiding envy

Everyone will get the reward of what he is doing if not instantly but in the long run. Because of this, you do not need to envy any internet scammer in your community. Even if he has built the biggest mansion in your community, it is not enough for you to be envious of him. Just lay low and stay cool. All that glitters is not gold so forget about the attractiveness.

He bought a new car of 18 million naira; and so? Is that the reason you are killing yourself? We know where the money is coming. They are eating the sweat of another man. The question is: are you ready to eat the sweat of another man? When the man has worked tirelessly by the day and sometimes part of the night, you receive his salary for him instead of him that worked for the money. That is wickedness written in capital letters.

How will you feel if someone receives the pay you suppose to receive after working for long? Will you be happy for that? If your answer is no, then let the scammers be. You have no reason to envy them because their conscience is dead. Some of them are not happy irrespective of their wealth. So, do not envy any of them in order not be tempted to join them. It is one of the capital approaches to avoid being a Yahoo boy or internet scammer. Enjoy what you legally worked for with peace of mind.

4.5 Who are duped by Yahoo Boys?

It is not everyone that fall victim to the tricks of yahoo boys. There are some set of persons that are likely or have already fallen prey to these fraudsters. Those who fall prey to Yahoo boys scam are:

The greedy

The unexposed

Illiterates

The poor

The get rich quick category

The greedy

Sometimes it sounds funny to observe how some people think. Some are very greedy and that is the reason they always fall victim to Nigeria internet fraudsters. You met an investor online and he told you that he had a project he was working on that if you can invest $5,000 in it you get your capital back with 150% interest within one month. Who does that? You are just so greedy to think the person is real.

You met someone online and he told you he has a large portion of land to sell for amount you know was much lower and you decided to send the money, you did that out of greediness. You want to harvest from where you did not plant. That is an act of greediness. The money the abroad victim sent goes to the private account of the yahoo boy.

The unexposed

Exposure is very important in the life of everyone living in this twenty first century. Always listen to things that are happening in the country. If anyone is updated and exposed to information and the trending things in the society, he is not going to be easily scammed by the Yahoo boys. Do not feel comfortable not reading news update and other information about banks.

When a bank sends notification to her customers, the customers should have time to read what the notification is all about. Some customers are too busy to read notifications from their banks. Some banks send messages concerning scam alert to their customers but many customers do not usually have the time to go through the contents of the message. That is why many fall victim. They are not exposed to useful information.

Illiterates

You will weep when you see some illiterate customers come to the bank to complain for their missing money from their accounts.

Sincerely you will feel for them. The author of this book works with First Bank of Nigeria Insurance and has had personal contact with some of these men and women. They come to the bank complaining helplessly concerning their missing money from their accounts. Some of these helpless illiterate customers did not know when they disclose their secrete information to these scammers. They come to the bank looking helpless and devastated.

Sometimes, those that do not know how to read and write fall victim of fraudsters trick. Because they cannot read or write and still have accounts in the banks, they do not know when banks send scam alert messages to them. They are like people who buy cars but do not know how to drive.

There are many account holders in many banks in Nigeria that cannot read or write. These are people that the officials of banks help to fill their accounts opening forms from beginning to the end because they could not read or write. When it was the time for the illiterates to sign on the account opening forms, they thumb printed with ink and sometimes sign with their initials to complete their account opening process. They do this because they may not remember what they signed before if they use something complex.

This category of people is easily scammed by Yahoo boys. A Yahoo boy may call any of them claiming to be a customer care agent from the bank he is banking. The scammer demands for secret information which he (the illiterate) does not suppose to give out and he gives such information out freely.

At the end, the fraudster dupes the man his good amount of money because he is not educated. There are occasions where illiterates came to bank and pitiably complain how they were scammed by yahoo boys by withdrawing their money from their accounts. Some of them laid curse on the scammers on hearing that they were duped.

The Poor

Some poor people in every society are always happy to hear any news that will make them maximize their money. People of this category if they do not discipline themselves can easily fall prey to the tricks of scammers. A scammer may call them and inform them that there is an ongoing promo and if they invest a particular amount of money in their scheme, they will get 100% return within one week. Because of the fact that they are poor and want to maximize their money, they fall prey to the tricks and loss their already hard earned money.

Poverty is bad. It makes people do what they may not ordinarily do. The poor think of how to make more money. They go to the churches more hoping for miracle to happen one day and be able to meet up with the demand of the society. As a result of this, any little thing can make them fall victim in the hope that it is the miracle they have been waiting for.

For example, there was a time when scammers used to call telephone numbers at random and informed people that they won a prize in one promo. Some of these scammers called and pretended they were calling from a telecommunication company.

Some called poor MTN subscribers and told them that they won two million Nigerian naira (N2,000,000). The poor receiver of the message feels happy on getting this call that God has answered his/her prayer without knowing it was a trick. The fraudster pretending to be an agent from MTN sometimes tell the victim that for them to pay her the money she won, that she has to go and pay five thousand naira (N 5,000) to an account.

The poor woman then rushed to the bank and pay into the account details given to her to claim her money. These guys are very intelligent Nigerians; pay five thousand naira and get two million naira. The poor woman calls after the payment for her payment to be confirmed. But little did she know it was a trick.

The Yahoo boy may say that they would get back to her soon. The next is that they break the SIM card after scamming other persons with the same line. The victim calls repeatedly and she could not reach the scammer. Her hope of claiming two million naira, as miracle, she expected is gone when this happened. What a world?

Poverty is bad.

The get rich quick category

So many people want to get rich quick. The get rich quick syndrome is all over the air. Some said that they do not gain anything if they do not make this money. In line with the saying, they want to make the money either by crook or by hook.

Many circular songs in Federal Republic of Nigeria are all about money. It is all about get rich quick syndrome. Some are doing a lot of dirty things because they want to make money.

It is a pity that because of this quest to get rich quick, many have fallen victim to Yahoo boys. Some have been duped by these guys because they want magic to be performed for them to make the money quick. Till today, many people who want to get rich quick are still victim of scam. It is painful but unfortunate they are trapped by their quest to get rich quick.

4.6 Funny Things Yahoo Boys do

There are many things that Yahoo boys do that are funny. These Nigerian young boys abuse the masses when they do certain things. We will be looking at some of these things here.

Praying to God to bless their Hustle

These young criminals pray very well. Can you just imagine that? They usually pray for God to bless them in their business. A part of their prayers goes in this form "Oluwa bless my hustle. Help me to pick today". Is that not funny? The word "Oluwa" is a Yoruba word which means God. Seriously, some of these guys have lost great sense of spirituality and religion.

How can someone who scams people to enrich his pocket be praying to God to allow some people fall victim to his tricks. These guys are really crazy as the author had not seen a situation where God support evil. God is God and can never be in support of people that dupe people to make money.

They now take Christianity for levity. To them, God hears them and can make them dupe more money from people. But that is not true at all.

Giving fat offerings in the churches

The twenty first (21st) century churches are so money conscious. Some pastors in the churches of the country are ready to collect large offerings from the G boys without asking of the source of their income. Some of them who know what they do to make their money do not even care. They are after the money.

Pastors who preach about tithing every Sunday forgetting to preach about the moral lives of the congregation wait every month for fat tithes from their congregation that are into scam. Christianity is losing its value today. Materialism has taken over the stage. Pastors and priests in churches in Nigeria are more interested in prosperity than the spirituality of the congregation.

During donations in churches in Nigeria, there are different categories of people that come out to donate. The category is dependent on how much any member of the church wants to donate. These G boys are usually in First Class category. They use their ill gotten wealth to intimidate others. Pastors and priests smile and pray for them as they make their donations. It is not as if these pastors and priests do not know what these boys do to make their money but their eyes are covered with the love for money.

The G boys give fat offerings in the churches with the mindset that more doors will be opened for them to pick more money. To some of them, they do not see what they do as scam but as games through which one can make money. Because of this ideology, they parade themselves in churches without any sense of guilt.

Some of them believe that giving such huge offering from the money they stole from innocent people will make their sins forgiven. As they are in churches, their minds are filled with the next deeper actions they will take into their dirty business. It is funny that some of them leave the church and find themselves into their dirty business again after about five minutes. Some even lost concentration if the church services take much time. They look good on physical appearance but their minds are filled with evils they will commit.

It is funny. They continue to make advancement in their criminal acts and later bring some part to the church for offering. The mentality of an average Nigerian Christian is nothing to write home about. Steal from people and take some to the church. They just go to church to show people they wear expensive clothes and went him to continue with their evils.

Anyone who works will make it

To them, scam is a work. It sounds funny to see a generation of youths that strongly believe that the criminal activities they get involved in is a work. In some of their discussions, you hear that anyone who works will make it.

In the other words, anyone who keeps on digging deep and advancing in fraudulent activities will surely succeed in scamming a lot of people and make money in the long run. They say to one another "as far as you keep working hard, someone will surely pay you one day". No matter what, one client will pay one day. That is what they strongly believe.

They do not see what they do as fraud but observe it as work. Because they have this perception that they are doing work and not something bad, they put in their maximum efforts. But no matter the name they give to it, scam is scam. Fraudulent activity is a fraudulent activity anywhere in the world. They call it work to cover up. But that is really funny.

It is done to a lot of them that what they have been doing is scam and not works but scam when they find themselves in the nets of security agents in the country. Some of these young men that find themselves in the custody of Economic and Financial Crimes Commission (EFCC) discovered that what they were doing was fraud and not work as they thought. Some till today are still in many prisons in the country without knowing whether they will come out alive or not. These boys that act funny should know that what they do is not work but scam.

4.7 Characteristics of Internet Scammers in Nigeria

Noise making

Drug Addicts

Womanizing

Extravagance

Restlessness

Noise making

G boys are noise makers. They like noisy environment. They derive joy in shouting at the top of their voices whenever they discuss in group. Their noise making attitude is a common practice they enjoy. Sometimes when people pass around them and observe them talking and shouting at the top of their voices, the people do not need a seer to tell them who they are.

When they come to banks to collect the money sent to them by

282

their victims, their tone are high. They can shout at bank officials if directed by the officials to do certain things right. If for example the Western Union official tells the G boy that the name they gave does not match with the name in his identity card (the G boy's detail) he can get provoked and shout at the top of his voice.

It is not as if the issue cannot be resolved but he felt like making noise to show the other bank customers that he came to pick money through Western Union. Shouting is part of G boys characteristics. They are noise makers everywhere in the country. Once some of them walks into the bank to withdraw the money sent to them by their victims, the staffs know. They make some kinds of noise and that creates awareness of their presence.

When the scam that brings the money is not engineered by only one person, there may be problem while sharing of their stolen money. The proportion to be given to each may be an issue. This makes them to quarrel right there in the bank and raise dust.

Have you been to a compound where G boys are living? If you

have been there you will understand what the author is writing about. Everything about them is noise. Even when they play music with their sound systems, they do that at high pitch. Even upon that, they still make noise as the music play.

Drug Addicts

Addiction is common among the youths and young fraudsters in Nigeria. It is only few G boys in the country that are free from abuse of drugs. As early as 1 A.M in the morning when they suppose to be sleeping, they are busy disturbing the people they are in the same compound with the smell of marijuana. Their lives are dependent on drugs.

Codeine and tramadol is part of them. The money they make through international and local scam get them intoxicated. This makes them behave abnormal. They combine different drugs they are not suppose to take just because they want to get high and feel happy.

Because of the drugs these youths abuse, they have the mind of doing what a person cannot ordinarily do. They dupe both the young and old without thinking of the repercussions of what they did. They do not think of tomorrow and are not moved of their evil deeds. They see evil as normal and what everyone has to do to survive. They say that every way is way.

A man who is in his right sense cannot just pick a knife, cut out the tong, the genital, eye, and breast of a lady all because of money. They become high before they can do that. They get high because they do not want to have any sign of mercy toward the victim. It is really sad.

Fraudsters are drug abusers. They get high and feel as if they are on top. They talk from one angle to another. They narrate stories on how they were able to dupe their victims' huge amounts of money. They indirectly damage their livers by drugs. If internet scammers can reduce hands on how they consume drugs, their atrocities will reduce. Drugs which they take reduce them to lower animals.

Do you know some of these young men who are into drugs today are victims of sexual transmitted diseases? Some of them are victims of Human Immune Virus (HIV) because they had unprotected sex when they were high in drugs. They find out that they suffer from AIDS when they go for test after long time sickness. Drug abuse is bad. It can make ones sense of how to do things right reduced.

Alcoholism for instance can have negative effect when it comes to reproduction. It can make a man impotent. It destroys some useful chemicals needed for impregnating a woman. But little do these drug abusers know about it. They drug themselves without understanding the adverse effects of what they are doing. There are problems in some homes today. What is the cause of the issue? Difficulty in child bearing is the reason for that.

Womanizing

Money intoxicates people. When someone makes money he could not believe he would make in his lifetime, such money can intoxicate him. He made the money through scam and it is so much. Before you know what is happening, he begins to misbehave high-time because he is intoxicated with what he has.

Today, you see him in a party with set of women and tomorrow you see him with another set of women. He continues that way all through his living as a youth. The money is there and that is why you see him doing all sorts of rubbish without rethink. He makes the money through fraudulent ways and hence lost sense of value of money.

But the trick is that some of these ladies they carry around do not know that their lives are in danger by doing what they are doing. Some of them have been used for ritual by the G boys unknown to them to make more money. They pretend to love the ladies but they do not know that something has been collected from their bodies by these wicked guys to make more money and grow richer. Some G guys are very diabolic but in coded way.

Some of them after sleeping with the women they carry to parties use handkerchief to clean the virginal fluid from the women and later take it to fetish experts that do ritual for them. The women sometimes remain barren forever or face nemeses all through their lives. They have ways they operate to use women for their diabolic rituals.

The one that happened recently in Shoprite, Warri, in Delta state of Nigeria made a lot of ladies live in fear. It taught them lesson that not all G boys they see on the street are nice. Some of them are devils wearing human skin. They are heartless and they are everywhere. It taught the ladies lesson that not every guy that dress in clean clothes and drive good cars are safe to follow.

That one that happened in Warri on November 2018 is an example. The victim met a guy in Shoprite who offered her N50,000 (fifty thousand naira) just to stick a finger in her vagina in the restroom of the supermarket. Little did she know that the Yahoo guy had interior motive. Immediately the guy sent N50,000 to her bank account she agreed without asking the boy any questions and went straight with him to the toilet. She came out with the guy after both of them spent about 15mins in the toilet feeling excited. After she escorted the guy to his car she went to her friend rejoicing (Cyril Okonkwo 2018).

After about 30 minutes of the G boy leaving the area, the lady who was fingered began to feel the urge to urinate. She then ran into toilet and began to urinate blood. She ran out of the toilet shouting at the top of her voice but the blood kept coming out of her virginal. It was dawn on her at that point that the guy that fingered her just used her for ritual for fifty thousand Nigerian naira only. She bled to death at Shoprite Warri. If you are a single lady and a Yahoo boy woo you, say no to him. Many of them are okay at doing evil because of their high quest for money.

Extravagance

They live extravagantly. It is part of them as they have their ill gotten wealth with them to always spend. They feel as if it is nothing and to some of them is nothing for sure. A situation whereby their clients send much money to them, they have much to spend extravagantly. Some of the yahoo boys are young and because of that lack the experience of what to do with money.

They go to parties and buy expensive wines and pour them on the ground. They pour the content of the bottles of wine on the ground to show the people that they have plenty of money. They have money they duped from innocent people to waste in parties. Some of them after pouring the wines on the ground decide to drink later. They are intoxicated with money made through fraudulent ways.

They enter supermarkets in the country and buy a lot of expensive items. They are indeed expensive and ladies who could not hold themselves are attracted by them. Some of them when in the supermarkets after buying the items may not even use them for a long time.

Some even give items they bought to use to other persons. This is after the items have stay in their houses for a long time and they feel they cannot use them again. G boys are married to extravagant lifestyle. They behave quite boldly, prove their social status in the online space and sometimes neglect the moral norms typical for ordinary Nigerian citizens. Yahoo boys publish photos of their expensive watches, cars and clothes. They show off.

Restlessness

So many Yahoo boys in the Federal Republic of Nigeria are restless. They are always afraid of their living. They do not know anything that may happen in the nearest minutes. Even when they are in social gathering, their eyes go to many places within few minutes. They are afraid of the evil they committed sometime ago coming after them.

When they are in their rooms and someone knocks on their doors, it takes them time to come and open the door. They are afraid because they do not know if the person knocking on the door is a police officer. Some are restless because they do not know if the person knocking comes with other people hiding somewhere. They may be attacked by armed robbers when they open the doors without proper observation. They are fraudsters and therefore live like criminals which they are.

There is no peace for the wicked. Because they are wicked by duping both the poor, the old, the rich and the illiterates to enrich their own pockets, they would never have peace. Some who kill to renew their diabolic powers and make them active again are living in fear. Their minds fly anytime they see the Corps or police officers. The reason is because they do not know if the evil they did have been discovered. Their hands are not clean so they are afraid.

Because of their evil deeds, some are restless when stopped at checkpoints by police. They are restless when police officers ask for their mobile phones to see what they have in it including their photo gallery section. The G boys may not like to hand their phones over because of the scam documents they may have inside.

4.8 How Yahoo Boys have Influenced Nigerian Security

It is a pity that those that are employed and established to shun crime are sleeping. They are like sleeping lions that cannot do anything good. They failed in their duties and cannot make any impact to make effective changes.

Policemen in Nigeria have familiarized themselves with these young scammers in Nigeria to the extent that they cannot talk to them as police officers. Instead of these officers to do their job by searching these young men and then charging them to Law court if found guilty, they are busy praising them when they drive pass police check points or even in police stations. It is a shame to Nigerian Police force in general.

Some policemen instead of arresting these G boys for defrauding innocent people are interested in collecting money from them at different strategic points. Those who are assigned in banks to secure the banks help left their fundamental duties and stand patiently at the gates of the banks waiting for any yahoo boy that comes out of the bank to beg for money. They are always eager to fill their pockets with money to be given to them by yahoo boys everyday. They lost sense of what they are sent to the bank to do.

Nigeria police officers have turned themselves to nothing because of the influence of these internet fraudsters in the country. Sometimes once these young fraudsters offer bribes to them while driving their cars and stopped at checkpoints, the policemen on duty allow them to pass.

They did not bother to check to find out if the yahoo boys are carrying exhibit in their cars. Some yahoo boys who kidnapped for ritual have passed police checkpoints freely because they influenced the officers with their ill gotten wealth.

Some yahoo boys who were arrested for one offence or the other are set free without adequate punishment because they influenced the members of the force with their money. Once they pay mouth watering amount of money to the top officials, they are set free.

The case is closed and no need for further investigation on the case that makes them find themselves in the sale. That is the attitude of some of the security officers we have in Nigeria. They allow themselves to be easily influenced by the young fraudsters in the society.

Instead of standing for justice, they stand for what is evil. They have failed both the government and the citizens of the country. Many yahoo boys are not even afraid of police again. Some of them challenge policemen at checkpoints for doing their duty. In European countries, fraudsters have no say but the reverse is the case in Nigeria.

In United States of America for instance, fraudsters tremble on seeing police but it is not so in Nigeria. Over there, they hide on seeing the officers on duty. But in Nigeria, fraudsters feel no atom of fear on seeing police officers. They know that if it becomes tough, they bribe them with money and then go their way. In United States, attempt to bribe a police officer is a capital offence but it is normal in Nigeria. Your money can buy you out in the country even when you committed a criminal act.

4.9 Why Many Nigerian Youths are Fraudsters (Causes)

Something does not just happen for happening sake. There are things that cause something to happen. There are some factors that make many Nigerians find themselves in that state today. It is a national issue. In this section of the book, we will be digging deep on the causes of Nigerian youths' involvement in fraudulent activities to make money for a living. The causes of Nigerian youths involvement in scam, hence called yahoo or G boys are as follow:

- High youth unemployment
- Poor moral training by parents and guardians
- High quest for riches
- Insatiability of Nigerian youths

High youth unemployment

Youth unemployment is the mother of many issues that youths all over the country have been facing for a long time now. It is a big challenge and has fuelled the involvement of many Nigerians into scams of various kinds. The belief If you cannot beat them you join them is what they decided to go into after searching for jobs for long time and could not get any.

Some of the youths may not like to find themselves into the attitude of scamming other people for money. But they became interested in the dirty game after being at home for a long time without finding any reasonable job. To keep life going and also to meet the demand of the society, they go into scam.

Initially, they might have structured their minds that nothing will make them to be yahoo boys of any form. They believed in themselves that they can make it on their own without soiling their hands into any form of dirty practices in the name of making money. As time goes on, they see their mates whom they know they were far better than then in school driving expensive cars and "doing things" in the town. The young men approach them whom are doing well in the society and to their surprise they are into fraud of different kinds both local and international.

After engaging the G boys in discussion to know the way forward as they who were waiting for jobs could not find any, they are trained into scam by their mates. They start doing fraud in the name of yahoo as they grow in level in the dirty business. Sometimes their conscience judge them but they moved on as they convince themselves that the reason for them doing what they do is because there is no job in the country. They continued to advance in scam in the country while the citizens who are not into scam tremble in fear not to fall victim.

Poor moral training by parents and guardians

So many authors that write in many genres were trained by their parents on how to do things and do them right. The author of the book you are reading right now is able to maintain certain standards in his life because he was well trained by his parents as well. He grew with the teaching to always do what is right and avoid doing what is wrong till he found himself into the field of writing on youth topics from his university days till date. It is a good one and moral practice was instilled into him right from when he was little.

The reason why many young people in Nigeria both the ladies and the guys are into fraud is due to the fact that they lack good moral training by their parents. They are poor when it comes to the area of doing things in ways that are morally acceptable. That is the reason why there is high moral decay in Nigeria today.

The youths want to make the money anyhow. They do not care to know if the channel they will use to make the money is dirty or not. It is all about making money. "If I do not make this money wetin I gain". That is the slogan of many Nigeria youths and it has been pushing them to do a lot of atrocities just to make money. It is sad that some of them do not know they will regret their ill actions latter in life.

A youth who is trained morally by the parents will not have the mind to kill a fellow human for ritual in the sense that he wants to fortify his diabolic power to be able to scam more clients for money. The fetish power of Yahoo boys came to be because many of them are very poor in terms of morality. According to Samson Ezea of The Guardian newspaper, "Yahoo boys don't have morality. They usually stop at nothing to deceive people and pocket their money (Samson Ezea 2017)".

Any person that comes from a good family where morality is practiced and cannot be done without understands the value of life. To such person, no amount of hunger for money can make him to kill. Life is sacred and should not be gambled with. Such person understands that no amount of wealth can be exchanged with human life. Whether the activities of these wicked men that kill for ritual is called Yahoo plus or not, poor moral integration is one of the reasons why they misbehave. Parents should take it as a point of duty to train their children on how to live moral lives to reduce the menace of fraudulent activities among the youths in the country.

High quest for riches

Our youths are getting mad for riches. Some of them can do anything for riches. They see the teaching of waiting for their own time to shine as old fashioned story. They want their riches today without waste of time of any kind. They want to wear expensive clothes, buy expensive houses and cars. They want to be praised by people. They always desire to command respect because of riches.

Because of the quest to possess such attributes, they go extra miles to get riches. If duping people can bring the wealth they want, they can do that without considering who is affected negatively. They do not care about who gets hurt in their quest to get rich quick. The attitude of high quest for riches has made our youths hide their faces in shame while doing what they cannot do ordinarily to make money when in their right senses.

"Yet, the cause of Cyber-crime in Nigeria as inordinate desire for wealth, you will find that a large gap exists between the rich and the rest of the population in Nigeria. Consequently, many attempt to level up using the fastest means possible. For any business to succeed, return on investment needs to be growing at a geometric rate with a minimal risk. Cyber crimes require little investment in time and money in addition to a conducive environment. Nigeria offers such environment and many cyber criminals take advantage of that (Kubiat Umana 2018)".

Insatiability of Nigerian youths

The word insatiability means impossible to satiate or satisfy. You have two cars yet you want to have ten with hundred houses. The more some Nigerian youths have, the more they want to have. Many of them are never filled. They are like oceans and hence want to be oceanic bank. Even Oceanic bank at a point liquidated and later joined Access Bank of Nigeria because they do not have enough capitals mandated them by the Central Bank of Nigeria. So no matter how much a Nigerian youth want to acquire, he can collapse one day if he or she does not take it easy. Fraud is not a good and no amount of baptism can prevent it from being what it is.

It is not as if it is a bad thing to desire for more but it becomes bad when one takes advantage of other persons because he wants to grow. That is wickedness and wrong perception on how to acquire wealth. There are people that have acquired many wealth today and they got them genuinely. So why dupe other persons because you want to make money?

If you desire to go higher in life, it is good and never a bad one. But do not do that at the expense of other persons that are working hard to make living. Imagine a situation why Nigerian Yahoo boy scams an advanced woman of hundred thousand naira and it took the woman about three months to save the money from the little trade she does in a rural area of one timid village. The Yahoo boy becomes happy for succeeding in the scam and the woman cries out for been a victim.

Insatiability is bad. Do not be envious of any person because you want to acquire what the person has. Be contented with what you have at your current level in life. It is time for our Nigerian youths to understand that no one will carry wealth to the grave. Let us be happy with what we have today and make genuine efforts for a brighter tomorrow.

4.10 Why Nigerian Government is not serious with the fight against Internet Fraudsters

We all know the truth. We know what is going on and fully understand why the government of the Federal Republic of Nigeria behaves as if they do not see anything wrong with the activities of the young scammers in the country. The government officials pretend as if they are doing something to stop the activities of Yahoo boys in the currently but critical examination will make you find out that they, the government, are not serious with the fight against these criminals in the country. They have their aims for

304

doing that.

High youth unemployment

Due to high youth unemployment in the country, many Nigerian youths find solace in internet scam to make money illegally and continue living. Many have really made money through this means and are really living large irrespective of the fact that the money is made through criminal act. But the government themselves sometimes see it as a game the way the G guys see it as a game and the way to make money by playing on the intelligence of their English abroad lovers. Their perception on what they do to make their money is totally different from that of the person who believes that moral lifestyle should be the priority.

Some Yahoo boys receive dollars from their abroad lovers every month. Because they have really worked on their women abroad lovers and seriously worked on their emotions as well, their lovers send money to them down to Nigeria anytime they are paid in their work places over there. In fact, some of the scammers who claimed

305

to really be in love with their lovers in Europe and America receive up to 40% of their women's salary every month. Once the abroad woman is paid her salary in a month, she sends the 40% of her lover down to Nigeria. She does this because she (the American lover) will not like to lose her lover to another woman. In her thinking, her Nigerian lover will come over and marry her one day.

Due to the trick of this kind, the fraudsters make a lot of money. Many of them make much more money than those who do legal jobs in Nigeria. That is the reason why many of them live extravagant lifestyles. They buy houses and buy expensive cars. They make money from their lovers that live and work in abroad.

Because the woman an internet scammer claims to love lives in abroad, they can have as many lovers as possible. Their communications are at distance and therefore communicate through the internet. The Yahoo boys take it as business while the white women believe that they have real lovers that will one day come over and live with them.

A situation whereby a Yahoo boy has five white women that pays him about $700 (seven hundred dollars) each every month, what is the need to search for Nigerian job again? When the $700 is multiplied by 5, it gives a total of $3,500 (three thousand five hundred dollars). The Nigeria equivalent of $3,500 is N1, 260, 000 (one million two hundred and sixty thousand naira). How many Nigeria jobs can give you such pay in a month? It is very hard to get unless top staffs in oil companies in the country. That amount of money is some workers four years salary in Nigeria.

The reason for the analysis is to show you why Nigerian government is not serious with the fight against internet scammers in Nigeria. Due to high youth unemployment in the country which the government have failed to tackle, the government sees the engagement of young men and women in the country into scam as means through which they employ themselves. That is called self employment. Because of this, the pressure mounted on the government by the youth as a result of job scarcity has reduced. The government pretends as if they fight these internet scammers but they do not really do that.

How many jobs will they provide for the hungry youths if they succeed in stopping them totally? This is what goes on in the mind of government officers in the country. They feel reluctant about the fight against internet scammers in the country and yet showcase to the world that they are doing something to stop the Yahoo boys in the country.

Reduction in physical robbery attack and other local crimes

Because Nigerian young internet fraudster are busy with their activities of extorting money from foreign men and women through their tricks, the attacks on citizens of the country physically has reduced. The behaviour of young men in the country moving into homes and injuring the victims because they refused to give what they demanded has reduced drastically. Some of these young men sometimes kill the people they attacked if they refuse to give the money they demand.

But with the emergence of internet scam among the youths of the country, the young men are busy working on white people for money. This has shifted their attention from attacking people physically because of money. The government of the country feels that because of the opportunity provided to internet scammers, they have little to worry about.

Before now, politicians are very afraid while travelling and driving around the country. Their fear is usually because of attack on them by G boys in the country. Since Yahoo boys began to dig deeper and make their money through dirty ways, the government fears less than former. Reason is because the 419 (the scammers) make more money and they do not focus on them (the politicians) again.

Kidnapping was on the rise before. The youths of the country sometimes target men who are well to do including the politicians. They believed that a huge ransom has the tendency of changing their lives to better. Sometimes it take them much time before they are able to secure and executive their plans effectively. Since some of these men are now into scams of different levels, the rate at which physical attack of this kind in the country is brought low. The young men and women have found another source of livelihood to them which is stealing from people who are financially buoyant through the internet.

Poverty reduction among young fraudsters

A young man who can buy a car of nine million naira (N9, 000, 000) is not a poor person. Irrespective of the wicked tricks these young Nigerian scammers apply to make their money, they are rich people. Some of them send fishing messages to the email addresses of their suspects and ended up getting the details of the people they target once the victims click on any of the links and register for one thing or the other. That is why it is not advisable to click on the links that are inside the massages of your junk or spam box.

Many of these young criminals in Nigeria are building houses in different parts of the country and the Nigerian government is aware that some of the money they used to raise the structures are made through scam and yet could not do anything to bring them to book.

They cannot act to stop the criminal activities of these young people because they, the government, know that the reason why these boys are into fraud is because they failed to provide enough jobs for them. Because of job scarcity in the country, the boys jumped into scam to make money and get alleviated from poverty.

But in general, that does not justify what they do as being right. Scam is scam but Nigerian government does not want to come out openly to fight the Yahoo boys because they know they have failed the youths of the country. They the youths do not want to continue to be in their state of poverty and therefore are making money either by hook or by crook.

How Nigerian government can take down Yahoo Boys (fraudsters) if they are serious

If Nigerian government is sincere to themselves and really wants to deal with the internet scammers in the Federal Republic of Nigeria, there are simple approaches they can apply to get the job done. There are things they have to do to break the wings of these young men and women that are giving the country bad name abroad and even within. They will stop their operations if they enforce the ideas to be discussed.

EFCC partnering with local banks

That is one of the capital approaches to adopt. The government of the country Nigeria need to charge this group to up their games. Economic and Financial Crimes Commission really needs to meet all local banks and discuss with them on how to get these guys down. But on the other hand, banks may not be open to accept the proposals of EFCC to get any of the Yahoo boys down.

Do you know the reason behind that? The reason is because staffs of the commercial banks in the country are friends to many young fraudsters in the country. They have familiarized themselves with these boys to the extent that they are good friends. Even the managers of some local banks in the country strike deals with the Yahoo boys before they are allowed to receive the money sent to them from abroad by their lovers or any person they scammed.

Before these boys are allowed to receive the money sent to them if it is much, they see the manager first to know how much they will give to him after the money is pulled through Western Union. It is a hidden corruption that goes on in banks all over the country.

But we cannot continue like this. A crime is a crime and the government of the country in her power have to put a stop to it. The EFCC should not allow themselves to be influence by these small boys that are giving the country bad names. They have painted the image of this country black. The government has to send EFCC agents to banks to work as undercovers among the staffs of the banks. Whenever the G boys come to the bank to catch the money sent to them through Western Union or Money Grams, they undercover should send signals to the nearest EFCC branch in that location.

When the team arrives, they interrogate the suspects to find out who they are. After that, they arrest these boys and take them to the appropriate places where they will face trials. This will help in a long way to stop the operation of the fraudsters to minimal level. Proper enforcement will yield positive results.

By the time these boys are arrested and face trials for some times, they will begin to adjust. At that point they will find out that what they have been doing is not game but a total criminal act. Bank should always supply information to Economic and Financial Crimes Commission to always get these boys that are messing up the country down.

Working with Police

It is true that the security sector of Nigeria has been infected by Yahoo boys in the country because they give money freely to the security men and women in the country which turns out to be bribe. Bribery and corruption is one of the major challenges in Nigeria and it has robbed the citizens of the country to a very great extent.

To achieve a good result in the fight against internet scammers in a particular region of the country, strategic ideas need to be applied.

Because the police officers in a particular community have familiarized themselves with the scammers, the first step is to transfer all the police officers in the areas where these fraudsters have their operations. The transfer will give room to bring in new officers that will work effectively without looking and the faces of the scammers. The transfer is to come as order from the government of the country.

Before the new officers arrive in their new areas of operation, they are educated on what they are going to the new area to do. They will also be taught on the techniques they will apply to track down the internet scammers. It will make their works in the new easier.

One of the ways to identify internet scammers in Nigeria is through the pictures they have in the image galleries of their phones. It is common with those that defraud white people through dating sites. They usually have nude pictures of their own or that of the person they impersonate. They have these pictures so that they can arouse their victims emotionally and get reasonable amount of money from them.

The police officers with the power of the government will be allowed to go through the phones of the suspected Yahoo boys. Any picture that has resemblance with that created by internet fraudsters will have the owner of the phone interrogated and tried by law if he is detected to be a G boy.

Also, the police will be mandated to visit hostels and homes in those areas. With this monitoring, students' internet fraudsters will reduce their dirty operations. Visitation by the special squad will make many student fraudsters quit from being scammers. It is a great idea that will reduce internet scam in the country. By the time many are arrested and punished for their fraudulent activities, others will learn their lesson. The punishment for internet fraud or scam includes spending years in prisons.

References

- Adunni .A. (2018), Alleged Yahoo guy dupes Oyinbo woman he met on Badoo N81m, check out what she did to him in Warri, published by Legit News, Nigeria

- Ahamefuna (2017), 2 Yahoo Boys Sell Lagos Lagoon To American Based Business Man For N787million, published by Nairaland, Nigeria

- Cyril .O. (2018), Yahoo Boy fingers Girl to Death in Warri Shoprite, published by Shoolsbiz Students Hot Joint, Nigeria

- Don Silas (2018), Fr. Mbaka exposes his impersonator before his congregation [VIDEO], published by Daily Post news company, Nigeria

- Federal Bureau of Investigation (2017), Binary Options Fraud, Published by Federal Bureau of Investigation, United States of America

- Kubiat .U. (2018), Causes of Cyber Crime in Nigeria, published by Research Cyber, Nigeria

- Lawrence .P. (2018), Avoiding Scams How To Protect Your Money, published by Commodity LLC, 1013 Centre Road, Suite 403S, Wilmington, New Castle, Delaware, 19805, United States

- Madaily Gist (2018), Top 10 Wealthiest Yahoo Boys and their Luxury LifeStyles (PHOTOS), published by Ma Daily Gist, Nigeria

- Oluwaseun .A. & Ruth .O.(2018), Ex-deputy governor's daughter allegedly used for money rituals by boyfriend, published by The Guardian News, Nigeria

- Osayimwen .O. G. (2018), The Celebrity Status of Yahoo Boys in Nigeria, published by Information Nigeria, Nigeria

- Perez .B. (2018), Corpse of missing DELSU student found without breast, tongue, published by Vanguard News, Nigeria

- Samson .E. (2017), Prevalence of Internet Fraud among

  Nigerian Youths, published by The Guardian News,

  Nigeria

About the Author

Okwuagbala Uzochukwu Mike P acquired his first degree in Metallurgical and Material Engineering, went through training on networking organized by Cisco Certified Network Associate (CCNA), and certified by the College of Insurance and Financial Management as a professional insurance agent in Nigeria. He is also a website designer, mentor to young people and youth motivator.

He once taught young Nigerians in secondary school. He is passionate to acquire new skills and that is why he reads and makes research to acquire unique skills in different areas of life. Currently, Uzochukwu Mike works as financial advisor in First Bank of Nigerian Insurance. He derives joy in writing helpful non-fiction books and articles.

Uzochukwu Mike has written over thirteen books that sale both locally and internationally. Also, he has written as contributor to powerful books which involve great scholars as co-contributors.

Example of the book that he contributed as a chapter author is WE THE PEOPLE: Building A New Democracy in Nigeria As A Model for Africa. The book is the product of a fine team of 18 distinguished authors who live in four different countries of the world; Nigeria, the United States of America, Britain and France.

Some of the books he has written on youths are: Basic Information in Youth and Youth Empowerment, Types of Youth Empowerment, Importance of Youth Empowerment, Youth Unemployment: Statistics and Causes, Guide to Youth Challenges, and Tips for becoming a Successful Youth. In computer, he wrote the title "Understanding the Usefulness of Computer in the Twenty-first Century". In the area of Metallurgical and Materials engineering, he has the titles: The Performance of Loofah Fiber in Mortar: A Pilot study on the Compressive, Tensile and Flexural Strengths, Metallurgical and Materials Engineering: Introduction and Applications, Powder Metallurgy: Its Engineering Consideration and Applications on Copper. He has written other books not mentioned here.

His voice is creative. His ideas are outstanding. His written articles are loved by readers from different parts of the world. His articles are not just combination of words but very informative as they are backed up with proper research works. He has been given writing projects by readers within and outside his country of origin and he delivered. You can confirm that his works are outstanding through his free articles on Hubpages United States on corruption, corruption in Nigeria, challenges in Nigeria, Kidnapping, just to mention but a few. His written works have been read by over 1.7 million people all over the world.

About the Book

Okwuagbala Uzochukwu Mike P picked it as a point of duty to write his first book on Nigerian issue after in-depth understanding of the society where he exists. In this book, he concentrates on the challenges that the youths in Nigeria face and the problems they cause to themselves and the country. Not only that, he suggested some practical ideas that can cause positive changes.

In chapter one, discussed is an overview on who a youth is. It also discusses the benefits of being a youth. Youths in Nigeria do not have much to participate in when it comes to politics. There is fewer number of them and that is also what this section of the book covers.

In chapter two of the book, the area of concentration is youth unemployment in Nigeria. The menace of youth employment has made many youths lose hope in the country. Areas covered in the chapter are: how Unemployment has affected the psychology of Nigerian youths, impact of youth unemployment on Nigeria economic growth, causes of youth unemployment in Nigeria, effects of youth unemployment in Nigeria, solutions to youth unemployment, and youth empowering organizations in Nigeria.

Chapter three is a trending issue among Nigeria youths from different parts of the country. It covers drug abuse among the youths in the country. The subheadings discussed in this section are: what is drug abuse, effects of Marijuana, other adverse effects of drug abuse in general, solutions to drug abuse among Nigerian youths and drug abuse in Nigeria tertiary institutions.

This book ends in chapter four and that is the most delicate topic among all the chapters of the book. There is no much written book on the title. In chapter four, you will be reading about the internet fraudster in Nigeria. These young scammers in Nigeria are often referred to as G or Yahoo boys. You will discover the tricks of these young boys who made their money early in dubious ways. Also, read the chapter to avoid being a victim of their scam.

Contact the Author

Email: pmicheal2013@gmail.com

Phone: +2347037278694